Operation
Violet Oak

First and foremost, to my wife Liz, whose unwavering support throughout was absolutely essential to my survival.

Second to my legal team, and in particular to Mark Crowley, without whose diligence I might have been writing this book from the inside of a prison cell.

Lastly, to all those who have found themselves falsely accused: may you find justice.

Operation Violet Oak

A Story of False Accusation

Stephen Glascoe

Seren is the book imprint of
Poetry Wales Press Ltd
Suite 6, 4 Derwen Road, Bridgend,
Wales, CF31 1LH

www.serenbooks.com
facebook.com/SerenBooks
Twitter: @SerenBooks

ISBN – 978-1-78172-579-5
Ebook – 978-1-78172-580-1

A CIP record for this title is available from the British Library

The publisher works with the financial assistance
of the Welsh Books Council

Printed in Plantin Light by Severn Print, Gloucester.

Contents

This Is A True Story

The events depicted in this book took place in Cardiff between the summer of 2016 and the autumn of 2019.

At the request of the Office of the Attorney General, the names of the complainant and other players in this book have been changed, along with a few minor details in order to protect the identity of the complainant.

Out of respect to the 'survivors', the rest has been told exactly as it occurred.

Prologue

A Quiet Day

I sit reading in silence. No birdsong, no traffic roar, even here in the heart of the city. No children laughing and shouting, no dogs barking, no insistent drone of lawn mowers or hedge trimmers. No ambulance sirens, no police helicopters hovering overhead, no magpies chattering. No noise from next door, though to be fair that is not unusual. They rarely disturb us, except when their young nephews visit. Clearly they are not visiting today. At this moment the only sound I can hear is the faint, ever-present hiss of my tinnitus. Normally I am easily distracted from it: by writing, carrying out household tasks, watching a film or television programme, or in conversation with others. I only become aware of it in times of repose: at night, while waiting for sleep to come, or at unusually quiet moments like this.

But there is the 'sound' of my thoughts. Psychologists talk of the 'internal monologue'. Buddhists see it differently: they speak of the internal *dialogue*, and even the most cursory examination of one's mental processes confirms this. I think I became aware of it when I was about ten, which was when I first realised I *had* a mind, and that probably everyone else had one too. We are forever engaged in a conversation with ourselves; one part of us 'says' something and the other part responds. The Buddhists say all thoughts arise from emptiness and dissolve into it in a continuous stream. The practice of meditation, they say, is no more or less than a 'listening' process, whereby we observe this endless arising and dissolving in a dispassionate, uninvolved way, dropping each thought the moment we are consciously aware of having it.

This sounds easy, but there's more to it than it seems. It takes hundreds of hours of practice to become proficient in dropping thoughts the moment they arise, until 'gaps' begin to appear where there are no thoughts, and all that remains is a state of undiluted, crystal-clear awareness. For those who have never meditated, or, like me, gave up the practice long ago, all we can hope is that the two entities inside our heads converse on an amicable basis, in other words behave like *friends*. Then we may be able to live in a degree of contentment. But all too often one side of ourselves berates, bullies and humiliates the other, and down that road lies irritability, depression and, in the worst cases, insanity.

At this moment my two selves are united in fear, facing a common enemy. In fear there is no conflict. I am reading, pausing every few minutes to exult in the silence and reflect that in prison, day or night, there is never a time when it is quiet. A friend who once spent time inside told me that apart from the fear of violence, it was the incessant din that was the most soul destroying. The banging and crashing, shouting and screaming, never stops. How shall I manage, should the worst come to pass and I am sent down for the rest of my life for crimes I did not commit? What if, in court, my accuser comes over as articulate, credible and sympathetic? And I come over as sly, evasive and unconvincing?

My hearing is gradually failing; that may be a help in prison, though not as much as one might think. As hearing loss advances, a phenomenon known as 'recruitment' develops. This is the medical term for the maddening experience of perceiving loud noises far more acutely than people with normal hearing. Many people will be familiar with the situation when one says something to a person with mild deafness which they do not catch, then repeating it more loudly, only to be rebuked with the words: "There's no need to shout! I'm not deaf, you know."

This is beginning to happen to me already. And perhaps I am being deliberately obtuse; everyone knows that far worse things happen in prison than it being a less than ideal place to settle down for a quiet read.

Perhaps I will be held in solitary confinement for my own protection. But is that not the most feared punishment of all, even by the most hardened criminals? Is not human contact essential for the survival of the human spirit? But I will still have books. Or will I? I have heard they ban hard-cover books; apparently the covers may be folded in a particular way to make a surprisingly effective shank. Perhaps they will allow paperbacks, but not hardbacks. That should be all right, but will they allow me the magnifying glass I now require to read most books? Could even that be viewed as a potential weapon? I have no idea, and hope with every breath I never find out. As I write this my future is being decided by agencies beyond my control. I can only wait, in a kind of breathless suspense, as the day draws near when I will learn my fate.

I should try to put this aside, 'park it', as they say, but it isn't that easy. There is my *past*. My behaviour, innocuous enough in my mind, but now adduced by the prosecution as an indicator of my previous 'bad character'. Trials like mine, where there is no hard evidence on either side, circle around such things.

"A doctor, yes, but a man of dubious character, a man who has admitted using illegal drugs, who counts drug users among his friends, can we really trust his testimony?"

My silk, his job is damage limitation, to put out fires. The prosecution's job is to blacken my name, the defence's to sow doubt, reasonable doubt, in the minds of the jury. Who will hold sway?

All I want is for justice to prevail.

But what if it doesn't?

Twenty years in prison. At my age, that represents a generous estimate of my lifespan. Of course time served is only half the sentence handed down, but in cases like mine parole can be jeopardised if the convicted continues to insist on their innocence. It seems inevitable I will die in jail, either alone, or sharing a cell with the kind of people I have tried my best to avoid all my life. Or in a hospital, handcuffed to my bed. Is that any way to die?

I return to my book in a deliberate effort of distraction, but before I have even finished a paragraph a great rush of fear washes over me like a breaking wave. My stomach churns, my face and hands break out in a cold sweat. I feel sick. All at once I am taking great gulps of air and my heart pounds. The only thing I can influence is my breathing: with a determined act of will I slow it down. Slowly the physiological noise melts away; in a few minutes all that remains is a slight tremor of the hands. Before long even that fades and I am calm again. This is my life now, and as my trial approaches I can only see the panic becoming an increasingly common occurrence. Should that be the case I shall have ample opportunity to practise my self-control.

I pick up my book again. Still it is quiet. My tortoiseshell cat has joined me, draping herself over the folds of my knees, her head hanging in space. Surely this cannot be a comfortable position for her, but it must be, because if I strain my ears I can hear her purring gently. I may be allowed books in prison, but I will certainly not be allowed cats.

I had better enjoy this while I still can.

Chapter One

Fear is more human than courage.
– *Svetlana Alexievich, Boys in Zinc*

Thursday, the fifteenth of June, 2017. Nine am. I should be writing about this. I really should. That's what friends keep telling me. "You're a writer," they say. "You have to write about it." And they're not wrong. I *should* be writing about this.

OK then, deep breath, here goes. The trouble is, I have been paralysed for so long now, unable to write a word through a mixture of fear, shame and guilt. Not for what I am currently accused; of that I am completely innocent, my conscience clear. No, I am feeling so anxious because of my unconventional background. My lawyer says not to worry about such things, but it will not be him on the stand. The prosecution will seek to paint me as some kind of weirdo; who consorts with shady characters; who cannot be relied upon when he protests his innocence. And to some extent it is true: my friends are drawn from all classes; some have questionable backgrounds. That doesn't make me some sort of sexual predator, a sadistic monster, so drunk on his power as a doctor he is capable of committing the most heinous acts imaginable against innocent children. It sounds ridiculous stated in those bald terms, yet that is precisely what I stand accused of, me, the most evil doctor since Shipman.

And I know, we all know, juries make mistakes. The media is full of sensational stories of sexual abuse at the moment; they could easily be carried away by these tales of horror and sadism, and I could go to prison for the rest of my life. A couple of years ago a friend sat on a jury considering a case of historical sexual abuse. He was horrified at the level of ignorance and prejudice in the minds of some jury members. Some had decided on the defendant's guilt on day one and refused to be deviated from this view despite all evidence to the contrary; another had such a limited command of English she repeatedly held up proceedings by asking for translations, this despite her affirmation that she spoke English fluently. What if I had a jury like that?

*

By a titanic effort of will, I am writing again. Even writing the sentence you have just read seemed to drain me like a marathon run in the tropics. Not that I know anything about *that*. In my thirties I ran a mile in eight minutes, just to prove I could, and I never ran again, except perhaps to cross a road in heavy traffic. Walk, yes, I can walk for miles, but a lifetime of smoking has left me with mild COPD (Chronic Obstructive Pulmonary Disease), so for many years the nearest I have got to running is watching athletics on television.

Sitting down to write is not being helped by the weather. 'Flaming June' is an expression all too rarely realised in this country, though in my teenage years I seem to remember my exam preparations being frustrated year after year by glorious early summers. The reality is that June, like August, often disappoints. But today southern Britain is one of the hottest places in Europe, with temperatures in the thirties every day and likely to continue for some time. George II once said a British summer could be characterised as "three fine days followed by a thunderstorm". Not this time. It being so unusual, Welsh houses are not built to withstand hot weather; consequently I am sweltering even in the coolest room in my house, while if I venture upstairs an oppressive blast of superheated air comes at me by the time I reach half way. Nights are unbearable. I have placed a large, powerful fan at the foot of the bed, which succeeds only in circulating pockets of suffocating air around the room.

I feel as if I am wading through treacle. Yet I used to love hot weather. I learned at school that Britain enjoys a 'temperate' climate, and I recall the disappointment I felt when the meaning of the word was explained to me. No extremes: no hurricanes, no tornadoes, few blizzards and even fewer heatwaves. A lot of rain though. It all sounded so boring. We can, however, be sure of one thing: the hot weather will not last. Soon it will rain again, that glorious, soft Welsh rain I have learned to love.

There are seven long months to endure before my case finally comes to trial, and many onerous tasks to undertake before I stand at last before judge and jury. Soon it will be the summer solstice, when the Sun begins its slow descent into winter. By the end of December it will be on its journey back into summer again. But at least I will have had time to write this memoir – if I can summon the energy.

*

Friday the sixteenth of June 2017, two pm. Cardiff Crown Court. The day of the 'PTPH' (Pre-Trial Preparation Hearing). Why no press interest? Some people accused of historical sexual abuse are photographed outside the magistrates' court as they enter, and again when they leave, and their story appears in the local, if not the national, media that day or the day after. Yet back in May after our initial arraignment at magistrates' court there was no press gauntlet to run; even more surprisingly, there is no one to photograph us today as we enter the Crown Court. One possible explanation occurs: just two days ago a terrible fire consumed an apartment block called Grenfell Tower in London. Scores of people were immolated, apparently due to the fire spreading rapidly upwards through recently fitted external cladding. My brother, down for the day from his home in Canterbury to offer moral support, offers this insight: "Of course you realise the cladding was purely cosmetic. It was just a prettifying exercise." A surveyor all his professional life, his words carry authority. Whatever the case, the media remains completely absorbed in the tragedy.

Once inside the courtroom, the five accused are jammed into a dock barely big enough for three. The heat is stifling. The smell of fear pervades the tiny space. Two take off their jackets; I want to do the same, but am afraid of the impression it might create. Through panes of one-inch thick glass (is it bulletproof?) we watch Judge Neil Bidder QC in action, clearly a man in total charge of his situation. At one point, while discussing the charges against me, he glowers over his spectacles at one of the prosecution lawyers and says:

"Charges two and five. They're a bit repetitious, don't you think? They don't add anything to the tariff. Just remove them and re-number the remainder, will you?"

The number of charges against me, at a stroke, go down from fifteen to thirteen. Unfortunately they are two of the less serious ones. I suppose that is good, but I am too frightened to appreciate the significance, if any. What remains is still enough to land me behind bars for a long, long time.

The next issue he addresses is the complainant's request that she use the services of an 'intermediary' when she gives evidence. Intermediaries are usually deployed when a witness has learning disabilities, and their task is to rephrase questions in simple, one-syllable terms in order to help the witness understand what is being asked of them.

"There's no evidence of the complainant being mentally defective, is there? According to my information she holds a university degree, and from a very good university at that. I have to say I am dubious about this request."

The decision on this is left for later. I hope her request is refused. If accepted the trial will be prolonged by days, even weeks, and every day in court will cost me thousands of pounds.

Judge Bidder explains that he will now ask the accused to plead guilty or not guilty, but admonishes us to think very carefully about our answers. If we plead guilty now, at this early stage, the sentences we attract will be considerably lower than if we persist in pleading not guilty and are then convicted. The accused are then formally asked how they plead to the charges against them. I go first. I look directly at the judge, and say "Not Guilty!" as each charge is read out, in as confident a manner as I can muster. The others follow. Everyone pleads not guilty to everything. It takes more than twenty minutes to complete the process.

The judge goes on to speak of a letter he has received from the wife of one of the accused, begging her husband's name not to be divulged because of the risk of their children being subject to bullying. The letter, much praised by the judge, invokes various human rights regulations coming from both the United Nations and the European Union. In the event he dismisses her request; there is an inalienable right, he says, for the public to made aware at this stage of the names and alleged offences of the accused. But he does urge the reporter, "and your editor" (there is just a single representative of the fourth estate present) to "use their discretion" in reporting the case. Clearly this admonition has been taken to heart. I am safe, for now at least, from being stared at, jeered or otherwise ostracised for crimes all of us have, to use the judge's phrase, "vehemently denied".

"There can be no doubt this is a complex and unusual case. But be sure, the truth will come out."

I nearly shout out:

"Good! That's what I want! I want it to come out!"

But I think better of it. I don't want to be done for contempt of court before the trial has even started.

Chapter Two

If you really need to escape the things that harass you,
what you're needing is not to be in a different place,
but to be a different person. – Seneca

Friday the first of July 2016. That was the day my life changed.

My wife and I were returning home from a four day city-break in Vienna. It had been getting steadily hotter all week. On the day of our arrival the temperature hovered in the upper twenties; by the Friday of our departure it had risen to thirty-seven. Blood heat.

Europe was still reeling in shock over the referendum result. At home the far-right was exultant, the far left also pleased, though less volubly so. Despite my own long-standing allegiance to the libertarian left, however, I have always believed in the European project, whilst acknowledging its inherent flaws. I awoke to the news on June twenty-fourth and found myself plunged into a state of deep dejection. And on our arrival in Vienna three days later, each time I saw the famous blue flags with their twenty-eight stars fluttering gaily from all the official buildings, I felt as though I'd been kicked in the stomach. Shortly, I thought, there would be one less star on those flags.

Trying bravely to put these thoughts aside, we did our best to appreciate the sights and sounds of this great European capital. In the heat of the day we would take refuge in the relative cool of museums such as the Belvedere Palace, and any other air-conditioned treasure houses we could find. Fortunately in Vienna there are many to choose from.

In the evenings, the heat still shimmering off the great boulevards long after dark, we wandered the streets of the Inner Ring, marvelling at the great Rococo edifices, like the Karlskirche, only a few hundred metres from our hotel. There we could sit close to the fountain with the other tourists and get some small relief from the heat.

For much of the time we were able to distract ourselves from the grim reality of Brexit that would be waiting for us at home. The media would be able to think of little else, I imagined, at least until 2019, when it would become an accomplished fact, and no doubt long after that.

The evening before our return I noticed a missed call on my phone. A police officer, one DC Cath Orford, had been trying to reach me. I called back; there was no reply. I left a text message saying I was sorry to have missed her call. I told her I was out of the country at the moment, but would be coming home tomorrow. I asked what the call was about. The following morning I got a text from her saying not to worry; she would get in touch again when I returned home. It was a bit unsettling; why would a detective be trying to contact me? But there were plenty of other things to occupy my thoughts, and the incident soon slipped my mind.

On our arrival at Bristol airport we were greeted by a delight-ful summer evening: clear blue skies; balmy air, though not as torrid as the Vienna we had left behind. A brightly coloured police car stood waiting on the tarmac next to our plane. I remarked to my wife they had probably received a tip-off about cigarette smugglers, having seen a TV programme called 'Nothing to Declare UK' based on this very airport not long ago.

I went through passport control and made eye contact with the official; I even tried a little smile. He gave me a slightly odd look; it was certainly not a smile. I moved through to a corridor leading to the baggage hall. My wife was a few steps ahead of me. At that moment I felt a hand on my shoulder, a powerful, bony hand, which swept me into a side room. And there, even before I had a chance to say a word, a pair of handcuffs were snapped on my wrists. Oddly, the first thing I noticed was that they were not too tight. One of the two plainclothes police officers in the room walked up to me, got right in my face and said:

"You were expecting us, admit it."[1]

"What? I wasn't. Why would you say that? I don't know what you mean. What's this about?"

"You are under arrest on suspicion of serious historical sexual abuse. Do you have anything to say?"

"I don't remember raping anyone, ever."[2]

I was told we would now be going back to Cardiff where I would be held overnight prior to being interviewed the following day. I asked about my wife. She would be informed of my arrest, though given no details. A search of my house would follow, under Section 18 of PACE (Police And Criminal Evidence Act). I stared at my handcuffs and said:

"Are these really necessary?"

"Yes they are. They are for your protection as well as ours." Perhaps they were worried I might harm myself, but they didn't expand on their explanation.

I thought of arguing further, but decided there was no point. I was taken to the police car and put in the back seat, the two police officers up front. On the way back they listened to their radio, not to the police waveband, but to BBC Radio 5 Live, which was covering the Wales/Belgium match, a quarter-final encounter at the European Nations Cup. Twice during the journey Wales scored. The cops cheered with delight. The first time, trying to behave 'normally', I cheered along with them. The second time I did not have it in me and remained mute.

On our arrival in Cardiff I opened the door of the car by myself: it had never been locked. I could have thrown myself from it at any point. So much for 'my protection'. In a small display of compassion, before we went into the police station I was allowed to smoke a cigarette. Perhaps there was a scrap of humanity about these people after all. Then I was put before the custody sergeant and the allegations read out. They were so horrible I stopped listening. If the name of my accuser was mentioned, it didn't register. The sergeant agreed with the detectives that because of the seriousness of the allegations, there were

1 My wife later told me they found her in the baggage hall and said exactly the same thing to her, and with a similarly obnoxious attitude.

2 My solicitor would inform me later he considered this an extremely poor use of words, though he was gracious enough to concede that I was under 'extraordinary stress' at the time.

grounds for holding me overnight prior to my being interviewed the following morning. I was frisked, my pockets turned out, my shoes, watch, phone and wedding ring confiscated. I enquired later why it was necessary to take my ring, and was told: "We had someone in once who swallowed his. It got stuck in his gullet and we had to rush him to hospital to have it removed. Caused a hell of a stink. Won't make that mistake again."

I was led into the fingerprint room where my finger and palm prints were taken. There is no ink these days; everything is digitally scanned. I was about to undergo a DNA test when a cheer came from outside. The officer dealing with me left the room for a moment, then came back grinning like a ten-year-old at his birthday party. Almost bursting with delight, he exclaimed:

'Yes! Wales won!'

The DNA test was forgotten.

I was taken to a cell for the night. It measured about three metres by two, equipped with a toilet (no seat), a nozzle in one wall for drinking water and a low bed, covered by a thin, but surprisingly comfortable foam-rubber mattress. There was a tiny skylight overhead, black by now because it was dark outside. It would never get dark inside: a bulb in the ceiling burns all night. I was advised to bang on the door if I needed anything, and then left alone.

How did I feel? The word fear sums it up best. A kind of all-pervading terror, though it was more than that. It was also combined with a strong sense of guilt. But guilt for what? I haven't done anything wrong. But guilt is what you are *supposed* to feel in here. The name of my accuser has not yet been disclosed to me, but whoever it is I am innocent. I am a 'normal' heterosexual; I have never felt any sexual interest in children. I have had a number of sexual relationships with adult women; not all of them ended well, though I never abused any of them. Cheated on one or two, it is true, but that isn't why I am here. So why am I feeling guilty? My wife has told me I look guilty even when I haven't done anything. My wife! How is she coping? Is she sitting on the sofa, weeping inconsolably, even wondering whether there could be something to the allegations, whatever they are? No. I cannot bring myself to believe that. She knows I am no angel; knows I have made mistakes in my life, some of them serious, but equally she knows I would never harm a child. The house will have been searched by now. How did she cope as she watched them sifting through our private property? What did they take with them? All these thoughts swirled through my head, murdering any possibility of sleep.

In normal circumstances I am a good sleeper, but I would challenge a certified narcoleptic to get a good night's sleep under these circumstances. I sat on the edge of the bed, walked around, lay down and closed my eyes for a while. Then I would sit up and go through the routine again. It must be getting late now. The sounds from other cells, the anguished cries, furious yells, pathetic whimpering I heard earlier had faded away. Occasionally I heard footfall outside in the corridor; sometimes the peephole in the door was opened for them to check I hadn't worked out a way to hang myself. After an indeterminate period of time I spoke to an officer performing one of these checks:

"Look, I know this isn't a hotel, but is there any chance of a coffee?"

A short while later a kindly-looking WPC handed me a remarkably good cup of coffee: strong, sweet, with a dash of milk, just as I had requested. As I drank it, I speculated as to how often it occurs that one night someone is sleeping on a magnificent bed in one of the finest hotels in Europe, and the next on a bunk in a police cell. It cannot be unprecedented, but it must be extremely rare. And now it had happened to me. Finally, exhaustion won and I fell asleep for a short while.

When I awake a glimmer of light has appeared in the skylight. It is morning, but as it is early July it could be only five o'clock: many hours before I am removed from the cell and my interview begins. I try to sleep again, but it is hopeless. I lie with my eyes closed, 'resting my eyes'. The officers checking on me every half-hour will see someone apparently asleep; do they know it is a sham? Do they care?

This, I take it, is all part of the 'softening-up' process, along with the handcuffs. Disorientate, isolate, enforce the feeling of guilt; that way, presumably, the guilty will be more likely to confess. It won't work with me, because I have nothing *to* confess, but it will compromise my performance at the interview.

Sleep-deprived, terrified, I will be easier to confuse, easier to catch out making contradictory statements.

Hours pass. I can hear the station waking up around me. I am allowed outside to walk in the exercise yard for fifteen minutes. Not to smoke, that is not permitted even though we are out here in the open. But at least I can feel the fresh air on my face. The area measures about ten metres by ten. I walk around and around the perimeter, reminded of Doré's famous engraving, except there are many prisoners in that image, whereas I have the space to myself.

Back in my cell at eight am sharp I hear a key turning in the lock and the heavy steel door swings open.

"Good morning sir. Did you sleep well?"

"Not really."

"Never mind. It'll all be over soon. Anyway, breakfast is served. Now, we have two choices: freshly microwaved lasagne or a very popular option we call 'All Day Breakfast'."

"Tricky decision. I think I'll go for the all day breakfast."

"Right you are. Tea or coffee with that?"

"Coffee please."

"Milk and sugar?"

"Both please."

The door clangs shut. A few minutes later my meal arrives. I manage two mouthfuls. In the tiny space the smell of it lingers for a considerable time. The coffee, however, is acceptable.

At last I am taken to the interview room where my solicitor is waiting. It isn't the man I asked for, but his appointee, who is not actually a solicitor but a 'police station representative'. His name is Alistair Coxhead, and his appearance is a little startling. He's built like an all-in wrestler; in fact everything about him is larger than life: huge, hairy hands, massive shoulders, a booming voice and an enormous head. My first thought is that he would be a good man to have alongside you in a bar-fight. He's sweating heavily, though that is hardly surprising. The room is stifling, airless, and almost fully occupied by a large pine desk with four chairs tucked against it. The whole atmosphere is oppressively, perhaps intentionally, claustrophobic. There are no windows; light is provided by the flat, unforgiving glare of a fluorescent strip. Now, nearly sixteen hours following my arrest I finally learn the name of my accuser, whom I shall call Florence.[3] Having not laid eyes on her for nearly twenty years, I can scarcely remember her. We chat briefly about the charges, which he says are obviously ridiculous. "She's using a scattergun approach", he says. "I can't see how anyone is going to believe all this."

Two police officers enter the room. One of them is a woman, who introduces herself as Detective Constable Cath Orford. After the interview I found I could recall little about her, beyond the fact she was female, probably under forty and that I didn't like the way she looked at me. She takes the lead in the interrogation, while the male officer sits quietly, taking notes. I remember even less about him, apart from not liking the way he looked at me either. Throughout the interview, a barely concealed aura of contempt seems to ooze from them.

It begins. DC Orford puts a number of allegations to me, each more hideous than the last. I am accused, *inter alia*, of digitally penetrating little Florence, forcing her to masturbate me, running my hands all over her body while laughing maniacally, and, worst of all, raping her. I am alleged to have abused her at a succession of parties at which she, and her father, were present.

"Did you know Ken D, Florence's father?"

"Yes, I think I met him back in 1984. He was playing pool in a pub I used to frequent, and we got talking. Later we became friends. He was a good man, very bright and warm too."

"When was the last time you saw him?"

"Not for over twenty years. We lost touch, then he must have emigrated or something because I haven't heard from him since."

"And did you attend any parties where he was also present back in the 80s?"

"I think so, once or twice. It's all so long ago, I can't really remember."

"Well, Florence can remember you attending these parties. That's where you did all those horrible things to her. She says you made her get on a table, stripped her clothes off and then made her sing and dance. She said you were all laughing."

3 Obviously not her real name: she is guaranteed lifelong anonymity, regardless of the outcome.

"No. Nothing like that ever happened. I don't remember Florence even being there."

"Did you know Mr D was a drug user?"

"Of course. He smoked dope all the time."

"Dope?"

"Cannabis, obviously."

"Did he use other drugs?"

"Not to my knowledge, no."

"So you say he smoked cannabis 'all the time', to use your expression."

"Pretty much, yes. In fact I warned him about it several times."

"Why did you do that?"

"Well, he had a persistent cough which I wasn't happy about, though he ignored it. He may have been in a state of denial about it. I don't know. Whatever, smoking dope, I mean cannabis, it was pretty widespread in those days. I understand it still is. And back in the day, a lot of my friends used the stuff on a regular basis."

At that moment below the table I felt my legal advisor's knee jab hard into my own. I looked at him and his eyes were flaming. He said:

"I don't think my client wants to say any more about that. Do you, Stephen?"

"No."

"OK, anyway, just one last thing on that subject, did you ever buy drugs from him, from Ken D I mean?"

"No."

"Did he ever supply drugs to you?"

"Well, if you class handing a spliff to somebody so they can take a drag off it then yes, but otherwise no."

"So you admit you smoke cannabis, Mr Glascoe?"

At this point my lawyer interjected again.

"As I think have made plain already, I don't see the relevance of that question."

"Actually I don't mind answering it. I have smoked cannabis once or twice in my life, but it made me feel sick so I usually tried to avoid it."

"OK, let me get this straight. You, a doctor, have smoked illegal drugs and consorted with a known drug user and indeed many others who smoked illegal drugs on a regular basis. Is that it?"

"I think that's what I've said, but I would like to say I try to avoid making moral judgements about my friends."

"We aren't interested in your moral judgements, Mr Glascoe. We're interested in what you've done."

"As far as Florence is concerned, I haven't done anything."

"So you say. But Florence says different. Now, let me ask you this: do you remember seeing Florence once when she was unwell?"

I thought hard. *Did* I do that? It is possible.

"Maybe. I'm not sure."

"She says she can remember it perfectly well; she says you lifted up her nightshirt and put your hands all over her body."

"No. That never happened. I would never do anything like that."

"Really."

"Really. It's a lie."

I think I can dimly remember the incident. I tell them that as I recall, I was careful not to come too close to her because when it became obvious she was suffering from something which was probably infectious, I didn't want to get the virus on my skin: I might be immune already, though the viruses might survive long enough on me for me to pass them on to someone else.

"So you admit you might have seen Florence in your capacity as a doctor. Was Florence one of your patients?"

"No."

I think about saying that although this sort of thing is discouraged today, in those days friends would often ask for advice about themselves or family members, even ask to be examined sometimes, and doctors would think nothing of doing what was really a very small favour. In the event I decide to say nothing.

"How about her father, Ken. Were you his doctor at any time?"

I think about this for a moment.

"I don't think so, no."

"I'd like to ask you about your juggling. Florence has told us you juggle. How could she know that about you?"

"Well, she came round to my house with her dad once or twice after my wife died, and I may have juggled for her; it's something I do for kids sometimes. Besides, it's common knowledge. Everyone knows I juggle. I've performed in public several times hell, I've even been on the telly doing it more than once."

"And what would else would you do when Florence and her father visited your house?"

"Drink coffee, chat, watch a video, that sort of thing."

"Smoke cannabis?"

"No."

"And juggle?"

"It's possible."

Why are they interested in my circus skills? What the hell has that got to do with anything? Then comes the next allegation: when she was fifteen, I, along with her father and five other men, participated in a gang rape.

"If anything happened like that I wasn't there."

"Florence says you were, that you had full sex with her and ejaculated inside her."

"No, it never happened."

They go on to ask me about my friend Owen H. What was my relationship with him, did he attend any of the parties, if so how often, did he smoke cannabis, and so on. I didn't want to land him in any trouble, though I did say I *may* have seen him at parties where Ken was also present once or twice. But it was so long ago I couldn't be sure. I have an excellent memory, but even mine does not run to retaining detail for parties I attended thirty years ago. The sweat is running off me. I feel I have no control over this situation. A disconcerting feeling at any time; at this moment it is absolutely terrifying. I notice myself starting to hyperventilate.

"So, according to you, what happened at these parties? Alcohol consumed, cannabis smoked, is that right? People were getting drunk, high, is that right?"

"To some extent, yes. But not me. I used to drive there, and I never drive under the influence of anything."

"But you've just told us you would have occasional drags on spliffs, and then you would drive home, so wouldn't you have been high then?"

"Off one drag? No way."

"What else happened at these parties?"

"Well, as I have said already, it's all a long time ago now, and my memory isn't perfect, but as I recall there was a lot of political debate. We often talked about sport too."

"Politics. Sport. And that was it?"

"Look, I can see you don't believe me but it's true. A lot of people who attended those parties were highly intelligent and skilled debaters. We would often talk long into the night about various political issues. I can see you're trying to paint them as some sort of Bacchanalian orgies, but they weren't. Not at all."

"Now, Mr Glascoe, Florence has told us she had been abused by her father for many years, but then his friends started to become involved in the abuse."

"Really. OK."

"She says you and others looked on while she was made to touch her father's erect penis."

"I never saw anything like that."

"She says on one occasion you came into the kitchen when this was going on and then you and all the other men were laughing."

"No, that just isn't true. I'm sorry, I hate to contradict the young lady but that did not happen. It's a lie. As I said, the incident you describe did not take place and it's incredibly distressing to hear I've been accused like that. I don't know how I can be any more assertive in saying I never saw anything like that happen."

"Florence has told us that because it was you doing these things and you were a doctor, she's never been able to trust a doctor since."

"Well if such a terrible thing happened I could entirely understand her point of view, but it didn't happen."

"I want to ask you this. You've said you like Ken D, that he was a really nice person."

"And very bright too. That was my perception anyway, though it is true that people show different sides of their personality to different people."

"We have a statement from his former partner, Florence's mother, and she describes him in a completely different light from how you describe him."

"That's hardly surprising. She was involved in an intimate relationship with him. And as I said earlier, in that case she's bound to have a different perspective."

"I'm going to go through a list of names and I want you to comment on whether you've got any knowledge of them. Starting with Owen H; well, you've already admitted he is a friend of yours."

"That's right, yes."

"Eric E?"

"No."

"Michael E?"

"No."

"Simon C?"

"No."

They proceed to name at least seven other men, some of whom I had dimly heard of, which I admit; the names of the others mean nothing to me.[4]

"I want to ask you one last thing: were you at any time Ken D's doctor?"

"I don't think so, no."

"In concluding, is there anything you want to add?"

"I'm very upset Florence has made these accusations against me; I'm shocked and horrified in fact. I can't understand why she would want to say such terrible things about me because nothing lewd or sexual ever took place between us."

And it is over. My property is returned to me, with the exception of my camera and mobile phone, and I am allowed to leave. Adding them all up, there are six charges in all: two of gross indecency, three of indecent assault and one of child rape. One by one, I have denied them all. It was clear the interviewing officers did not believe a word I said. Their body language and skeptical looks said it all. Yet even now, I haven't realised what is going on here. I know I have been accused of hideous crimes against a young girl, but at this moment, in my *mind*, I am still 'helping the police with their enquiries'. It still hasn't occurred to me that the police were using their considerable skills to trap me into making a mistake, contradicting myself in a way that will

4 I later found out several of these men had died years ago.

appear suspicious when the transcript is read out in court. And it worked. I ended up saying a number of unwary things that might indeed embarrass me later on. I don't say anything to my legal advisor; presumably he knows what he is doing, but I find myself wondering if it might have been better to give a 'no comment interview', while noting all the questions carefully, and then issuing a statement denying all the charges. I've seen enough police procedurals on television to know this often happens. Then I wouldn't have got in a fix about the drugs, and other things as well.

Finally I am released on police bail, warned against contacting the 'complainant', her mother, her sister, her brother, the other accused men, and finally, ordered to answer bail in three months. Ken's name is not on the list, so presumably they haven't found him yet. My guess is that he left the country years ago. He may have died. I have no idea. But Owen's name *is* on the list. My God! He's been ensnared in this too! That's why they were interested in our relationship. It is stunning to me.

Mr Coxhead drives me home in his battered SUV which, I notice, is filled with surfboards, wetsuits and a mountain of other gear. The surfing solicitor! I am already overwhelmed by a sense of total unreality; this puts the seal on it.

On the way home I have a sudden thought.

"You know, thinking about it, maybe I *was* her father's doctor for a while."

"I wouldn't worry about it if I were you. I don't think it matters."

Finally I am reunited with my wife. I cannot remember ever seeing her so grey. I probably look no better, but she is too discreet to say anything. I pour myself a very large whisky.

We have another drink. Liz is smoking a cigarette. Liz! In the twenty-four years I have known her, I have seen this on only a few, a *very* few occasions. I ask her what the police seized following the search of our house.

They took very little with them, apparently: my computers, one of which was a glossy laptop I had bought only two months before, a huge batch of family photographs, and a battered old address book I've had since my twenties, and constitutes as good a history of my adult relationships as you could wish to find.

They were in and out within half an hour, she says. And, interestingly, their attitude was almost apologetic.

As we begin to relax a little, it comes to us both at the same moment. The party! We are holding a party here in just seven days; we have already invited thirty of our oldest and dearest friends. What are we going to do? Shall we cancel? Surely it is too late now. It occurs to us to put a notice on the door on the day of the party:

PARTY CANCELLED DUE TO FAMILY EMERGENCY
WILL CONTACT YOU LATER
SORRY ABOUT THIS
LIZ AND STEVE

But people are bound to smell a rat. My friends aren't stupid. After a lot of agonising, we decide to go ahead. How hard can it be? All we have to do is pretend nothing has happened for about five hours.

The following day we hit the local supermarket and stock up on party stuff. We book a selection of Indian snacks from a nearby curry house. The effort required drains every ounce of our energy. But then even walking up a flight of stairs has the same effect. I feel I have aged thirty years in a weekend. Will we be able to fake it? I can't see how.

When I worked as a GP I would often advise patients to fake being OK even when their lives were in turmoil; for their children's sake, for their colleagues' sake, for their own sake. "If you can fake it you're already halfway there," I would tell them. Now it is time to take my own advice, something always easier said than done.

Somehow the party goes off without a hitch. I look at my friends and keep thinking:

You know me, *you* would never believe I could be capable of such horrendous crimes. I'm going to need your help soon. Over the course of the summer, one by one, I am going to have to contact you, tell you the story and hope you will write a letter of support for me. And you will do it, because you *know* me.

Afterwards we wonder if anyone noticed anything strange about our behaviour that night. Some of our friends are highly perceptive. But no one says anything. I cannot help wondering, however, whether later, conversations along the following lines might have taken place:

"Darling, did you notice anything odd about Liz and Steve last night?"

"How d'you mean?"

"I don't know, there was just something, you know, *off* about them."

"Come to think of it, I think there was too, but I couldn't put my finger on it."

Whatever the case, looking back on that night I decide that however long we live, we can count getting through that party among our finest achievements.

Over the next two months, I contacted nearly twenty of my friends, almost all of whom had attended our party, to ask them for their help. No one declined. And no one noticed, or at least *said* they noticed, anything unusual about our behaviour that night.

Only a few days after this my wife and I had a furious row, the first in many months. The cause: attempting to apply flea medicine to one of our cats. I was charged with holding her still while my wife applied the drops to the nape of her neck. But cats can be incredibly strong when they know something is afoot, and she escaped from my grip, scratching me deeply on the back of one hand in the process. Liz screamed at me:

"What's wrong with you? Why couldn't you keep her still?"

"Me? Why didn't you put the drops on straight away, when I'd got her?"

"Oh, right, it's my fault, it's always my fault, isn't it."

"Well, it was this time. You fucking idiot, why do you always freak out when all you need to do is remain calm?"

At this point she burst into tears and rushed out of the room, weeping loudly. I yelled my apologies at a slammed door. I stood there, blood dripping from my hand, thinking: this is intolerable. We can't allow this sort of thing to happen. Not now. The stress is bad enough already without making it even worse for ourselves. I stood motionless for a long time, feeling utterly wretched. Finally I sought her out, apologised again and this time she apologised too. We made friends again and resolved to keep it that way for as long as it took.

I had met Liz in 1993, interestingly enough, at one of Owen's parties. At the time I was a single parent, having lost my wife to breast cancer three years before. I was immediately struck by a number of distinctly pleasing things about her. The first thing I noticed was her décolletage; the second her tiny waist. Later she would tell me she ascribed this to playing the oboe. Whatever the truth, and in the past my only knowledge of oboe players was that they seemed to expend such immense effort drawing notes from their instrument they always seemed on the verge of apoplexy, all I knew was that her waist was slender enough to arouse the envy of a Catherine de Medici. Second was her face. Her *gamine* features, her clear blue eyes, her dark hair cut into a bob, all of this gave her a more than passing resemblance to Louise Brooks.

But what struck me most on that first encounter was the fact that, despite obviously having had a great deal to drink, she was still able to acquit herself most formidably at Trivial Pursuit. I remember thinking at the time, if she can pull off a performance like that despite being seriously pissed, she must have a lot going for her. We started dating soon after, and living together not long after that. My original assessment of her character proved only too accurate. Best of all, she took to her role of surrogate Mum to my six-year-old son, or 'quote-marks Mum' as we called her, surprisingly well. In some ways she was a better parent than me; certainly she carried less emotional baggage than I did, and more important, was far more patient with him than I was.

It quickly emerged we had a great deal in common. We both played a number of sports, and enjoyed watching sport on television just as much. We both liked reading and the cinema, and favoured 'busy holidays', preferring to visit museums and ancient monuments rather than lazing about on a beach or in a bar. And our qualities appeared to dovetail as well. My medical training has taught me to cope well in a crisis, while she could be prone to panic sometimes. And whereas her mind was ideally suited to carefully considered analysis of any given situation, I was all too easily inclined to make snap decisions which were sometimes of poor quality. A Lebanese friend, having spent a little time with us, expressed his envy at the strength of our relationship, in stark contrast to the sometimes chaotic nature of his own. "You're like a team," he said. "You work so beautifully together."

Not that we never quarrel, though there is nothing wrong with that. As Fay Weldon has observed, there are occasional explosions of anger in even the best ordered of families, and I have always thought there must be something wrong with the couple that never argues at all. At this moment, however, there must be no question of conflict. We are united by the threat posed by a mighty enemy: the State. We must show total solidarity if we are to prevail. This is her disaster as well as mine, even if she shows great expertise at concealing how much it is affecting her. From a purely selfish perspective, the fact that she is my ally is giving me enormous succour at what must be the most dangerous time of my life. As each day passes I find myself leaning on her more and more, and can only hope she holds up under the burden of keeping me afloat.

Chapter Three

Fear is almost indistinguishable from grief
— *Javier Marias, A Heart so White*

Saturday, the second of July, 2016, two pm. Overnight my drinking has doubled, as has my cigarette consumption. When I lost my wife in 1990, when I lost my son in 2006, I calculated that a cigarette appeared to make me four per cent happier. Now, as then, I find myself attempting to be four per cent happier anything up to six times an hour. The alcohol seems to make no difference at all, but I drink anyway, almost as an automatic response. I spend hours sitting in a kind of numbed haze, smoking and drinking, drinking and smoking, staring at the TV screen, seeing nothing.

In response to a major trauma, the human body produces a surge of endogenous steroids. Probably some kind of survival response, this has a number of effects. My chest condition improves, and my eczema melts away almost completely. I remember this happened, first when my second wife died, and then again sixteen years later, when I lost my son. Now it has happened again. From experience I know it will take many weeks for the effects of the steroid surge to recede.

In the week after my arrest I went to meet my solicitor, Mark Crowley, accompanied by my wife. She will be by my side throughout all this, except when the barrister excludes her from meetings because she may be a witness and must avoid being 'tainted'. If I was hoping to feel better after this first meeting I would be disappointed. My first notion to be disabused: that the investigation might be dropped due to lack of evidence.

"I don't get it. If it's only her word against mine, and there aren't any witnesses, how can they take it forward?"

"I'm afraid you are under a misconception. That may be the case in most crimes, but in historical sexual abuse the onus is

34

now on the defendant to prove his innocence, rather than the other way round. This has been referred to in some quarters as 'the feminisation of the justice system'."

Until recently, he explains, corroborating evidence, DNA for example, or torn clothing, used to be required. This is no longer the case.

"What about the fifty per cent rule?" I asked, referring to the CPS's (Crown Prosecution Service) policy of only prosecuting cases when they believe there is a greater than fifty per cent chance of a conviction.

"Not in these cases," he replied. "These days, following Savile, they tend to wash their hands of responsibility and simply put them all to a jury for them to decide. That way neither they, nor the police, can be accused later of not taking a complainant seriously. Then of course there is the fact that you are a doctor. Obviously these crimes are horrifying whomever is alleged to have committed them, but society takes a particularly dim view of a doctor crossing a line."

Afterwards my wife told me that this is when I started to go pale again.

"These cases often revolve around 'bad character'. And in your case, with your being friends with the complainant's father, who, according to the police at least, was not exactly a pillar of the community, the prosecution will push hard to put it before the jury. You also admitted to smoking cannabis yourself, which is a trifle unfortunate. We'll try to counter that, naturally, by saying that that is neither here nor there, and has no bearing on the case, but... What you need to do now is to collect statements from your friends, former patients, relatives, whoever, in support of your previous good character to balance that."

At this stage I imagine I went an even whiter shade of pale, even though this was a contingency which had already occurred to me. Only a few friends know about my connection with Ken, Florence's dad. Unfortunately the police appear to be among them. My lawyer tried to lighten the mood before we left by saying he still felt I had a good chance of acquittal.

"In the Crown Court, a high standard of proof is required, and juries are reluctant to convict on the basis of one person's uncorroborated testimony."

But then it went sour again when he warned me that if found guilty I could face a sentence of up to fifteen years. We walked the half-mile home in dead silence.

*

My house has been searched, my computers seized. Doubtless they will be disappointed when they don't find what they were looking for: pornographic images of children, my history showing I have visited forbidden websites. Research has shown almost one hundred per cent of paedophiles visit these websites regularly and also keep vast collections of child porn, or 'spank-banks' as they are sometimes called. Absence of any such images on a suspect's computer should immediately cast significant doubt on their guilt. Conversely, if none was found on any of our devices it would be powerful exculpatory evidence. They will also be looking for any signs I had been in contact with my fellow-accused, but again they will be disappointed, except for my already admitted friendship with Owen. And I made no attempt to hide that in my interview:

"I've known Owen for thirty-five years. He is one of my oldest and dearest friends," I told them.

Now I am barred from speaking to him 'in any way, including electronically', as it states in the bail conditions. A quaint phrase that; it seems to come from another era. I still think of him at least twice a day: when using shampoo, which he always advised I should use minimally, if at all, and when using the loo at night. I always used to stand there, even at three in the morning, until he advised me to sit down. That way I could more easily drowse, stay closer to sleep than if I maintained a standing position. What an invaluable life-tip! It changed my life for the better in a small but crucial way. If nothing else (and there is so much, so much else), for that alone I shall always be grateful to him. But now my relationship with him has shrunk to these minuscule propor-tions.

The other day I found myself thinking about him, and my mind journeyed back more than thirty years to the magical summer of 1986. In the spring of that year we had discovered the 'Aerobie' or flying ring. It has set records for being hurled prodigious distances.[5] Made of soft rubber and thrown like a Frisbee, it can be propelled much further than the latter, and when we found ourselves consistently throwing it beyond the confines of our nearby playing field and into the surrounding roads, we realised we had to find a larger venue. We did, and after a little practice we found we were able to stand more than two hundred yards apart to launch the "ring" as we called it, towards our partner. If it was thrown perfectly, the ring could land in the other's hands without the need to take more than a few steps to gather it, despite its being airborne for anything up to thirty seconds. Rather more often it would carve a massive arc in the air and we would have to sprint as much as fifty or sixty yards to make the catch. But this was in the years before I developed my lung difficulties and I was able to achieve these sprints many times before becoming fatigued. Looking back, I now realise that as that summer progressed I was becoming fitter than at any other time in my life. On almost every fine day when we weren't working we'd be out in the park with our ring.

As the weeks passed and our proficiency increased, we devised new ways of catching, under the leg, behind the back and so on, as well as different ways of throwing, using the unorthodox 'forehand' throw in addition to the more usual 'backhand' technique familiar to frisbee throwers. They were days of great joy.

The point about this activity was that it was co-operative rather than competitive, and I think now it was that aspect which appealed to us most strongly. We had met about four years earlier and discovered we had a lot in common, in particular our political views and a love of sport. We were both quite skilful in a range of activities and competed for all we were worth. Owen was my superior in badminton and snooker, while I had the edge in tennis and table tennis. In everything we were passionate about winning, and, naturally enough, hated to lose. We were also competitive intellectually. Both of us were of above average intelligence, neither one noticeably brighter than the other, and we both had a tendency to be highly assertive, even dominant in debate. As a result we would sometimes clash violently; indeed, because of these clashes, throughout the course of our long

5 The current record, incredibly, is over a quarter of a mile

friendship there have been several lengthy periods when we were not on speaking terms. But we have always been able to repair the damage. Until now. Now we are estranged once more, though this time it is due to agencies beyond our control. "Let's go fling the ring!" we used to say. God! How I wish I was flinging the ring with him now, instead of living in this hell day after day.

*

The police will be disappointed if they are looking for any hard porn on my computer, though they will find my extensive collection of images of Hollywood stars, all the way from Clara Bow and Jean Harlow, through Claudette Colbert and Carole Lombard, to Elizabeth Taylor and Sophia Loren. They will find them in a folder named 'Sirens of the Silver Screen'. What will the prosecution make of them? It isn't hard to imagine:

"This man is a pervert. Clearly someone who does not respect women, despite his protestations that he does respect them and is even a feminist! Would a feminist have such a vast collection of images which objectify women, members of the jury? I think not."

"And why do you keep so many of these images on your computer?" I will be asked when I come to give evidence.

"I have an interest in the cinema which goes back to my childhood", I could reply.

"Well you've certainly had an interest in glamorous and often partially clothed women since your childhood."

"I wasn't aware that was a crime."

Maybe I will get a chance to add "I don't see how that makes me a paedophile, or a child rapist". And perhaps I will be told that I am there to answer questions, not to make statements. And that the jury will draw their own conclusions from my collection of 'obscene' images. Maybe all this is absurd paranoia. Maybe not. Maybe I am simply going quietly insane. The fact remains I am in such a desperate state at this moment I am seeing potential threats in almost everything.

Then there is my creative writing portfolio. In amongst it they will find my autobiography, written some years ago. In its pages they will find my accounts of experimentation with drugs back in my teens and twenties: marijuana, magic mushrooms, the time in 1976 when I took LSD in San Francisco. I don't think there was any drug I didn't try at that time, and write about, heroin included. I can argue that there is a long history of doctors testing the effects of drugs on themselves, as a form of 'field research', but all I can hear in my head is the prosecution barrister chanting the words bad character, bad character, over and over like some hideous mantra. More paranoia? I don't know. But I do know I'm so worried about it I haven't even told my solicitor yet. Perhaps I should: maybe he'll tell me there's nothing to worry about and I can start to feel better. On the other hand he might turn pale and murmur "Oh dear! This is going to a problem."

Every day, every hour, these thoughts have been going through my head without respite. They stop me reading, writing, watching the television. They pervade my walks and wake me from my sleep. My wife is probably having the same thoughts, though she has the discretion, for the most part, to keep them to herself. To tell the truth, she's been fantastic.

In the weeks following my arrest I found myself studying my hands and wrists constantly. I have never much liked my face. It has an out-of-proportion nose, sloped-back forehead and receding chin, but I have always liked my hands, particularly since, in my twenties, a girlfriend described them as 'beautiful'. I do not have particularly long or graceful fingers; they are not a pianist's hands, but the whole effect is still pleasing; even now, when the backs are traced across with fine lines and stippled with age-spots. The preoccupation with my hands and relatively slender wrists persisted for many weeks. To be shackled like a common criminal! Why did they do it?

What a wonderful gift freedom is, and how effortlessly we take it for granted. I remember saying to my wife in the weeks following my arrest that if at the end of all this I was acquitted on all charges I would never have another unhappy day in my life. It occurs in retrospect this was perhaps a little unrealistic or even foolish, but in all seriousness, what else could possibly happen to me that in any way compares to this? I have lost a wife; I have lost my only son. Those two life events surpass even this in terms of emotional impact, but not by much. Losing my freedom for perhaps the remainder of my life, for crimes of which I am completely innocent: in all candour, what else could happen to me which would even come close? To be unhappy after being exonerated of such terrible charges would itself constitute a crime against freedom.

Somewhere in the deep background events are happening in the world. A Prime Minister has resigned; another has assumed office. Inside the Tory party, vicious power struggles are underway. In Syria Assad continues to wage war against his own people. In nearby Palestine the settlement-building is proceeding apace, whilst on the other side of the Atlantic Hillary Clinton is embarrassed by revelations concerning her use of a private email to send state secrets. Will it damage her chances of matching her husband's achievement? Donald Trump, for his part, is holding onto his dream of becoming the first private citizen ever to become President. But it is all so remote from my life it seems as if it is happening on a distant planet, or in the pages of a history book...

Chapter Four

You've got to have a bit of stress in your life. Otherwise
you'd never get out of bed in the morning. – *Prof N.C.H. Stott*

Friday the eighth of July 2016, six am. I wake whimpering. I was
dreaming. In my dream, I am in the front room of my house,
speaking to my cleaning lady. It is broad daylight. She stands tall,
silent, stomach in, chest out, shoulders back, regarding me with
a look of utter disdain. Suddenly the room goes completely
black. Terrified, I cry:

"What's happening?"

I can no longer see her, but I know she is still there. I fall to
the ground and weep.

"What's going on?" I scream. "Why is this happening?"

Awake, I remain in a kind of dulled state for hours afterwards, sodden with the dream. I have had another dream
recently, and this one recurs constantly. I am on board some sort
of ship, and the captain has ordered the passengers to make their
way through an incredibly small gap in the deck. I can see others
squeezing through with great difficulty. Then it is my turn. I look
at the gap. I look at the captain. He gestures that I should go now.
But the gap is smaller than my body: it is impossible. I kneel
down next to the gap; even my head will not fit in there. I wake
up.

All at once my joy in watching sport on television has evaporated. During the early rounds at Wimbledon, I watch as the
camera pans over the crowd and find myself thinking: *you're* not
in as much trouble as me, *you're* not in as much as trouble as me,
Christ, *no one* is in as much trouble as I am right now. Someone
on trial for rape and murder maybe, or a family in Aleppo whose
home has been destroyed and their children blown to bits or

lying in hospital beds covered in blood. Perhaps *they* are, but it's a close-run thing. Perhaps a closer analogy might be a political prisoner, thrown in jail for crimes no more serious than protesting the injustices of a tyrannical state. But the closest analogy of all would be the growing number of people in this country who, as I write, are languishing in prison, falsely convicted of sexual crimes.

Come on, I try to tell myself, it isn't that bad. You might be found not guilty. But I will have to endure the adverse publicity, the daily coverage which will probably go national, when in the opening weeks of the trial Florence takes the stand and catalogues her terrible accusations against me. As the weeks pass I come to see that even these things pale into insignificance against the main issue – I *must* be found not guilty on *all* charges. Only then can I live out the remainder of my life in a degree of peace.

I watch Murray win the Men's crown for the second time; it hardly registers. When he won it for the first time in 2013 I whirled around my living room in an ecstatic dance of victory, I feared I might never live to see a Brit win tennis's greatest prize, and when it finally happened I experienced a sense of consummation I have rarely if ever felt before. This time, I could hardly have cared less.

Later at the Olympic Games in Rio, again an event that has thrilled me since the Tokyo Games of 1964, I watch the footage with scant interest. I'm in trouble; more trouble by a long way than I have ever been in before, and a lot of people running round a track or hurling things as far as they can barely arouses my interest.

On the television I watch chat shows such as Graham Norton's and find myself feeling an increasing sense of envy and almost hatred towards his high profile guests. As, one after another, they radiate their air of overwhelming self-confidence I think to myself, yeah, you can be like that now, but I bet you wouldn't be quite so full of yourselves if something like *this* was happening to you.

★

Monday the first of August 2106, ten am. One month on from my arrest. Everything has gone quiet. I seem to be spending the whole time sighing. Or yawning. I read a book, watch a TV programme and find for several minutes I haven't thought about my little problem. Then I do. And sigh. Or yawn. Eventually even this seems to settle down. After six weeks my wife and I are slowly returning to a state resembling, but in truth very far from, normality.

I go through each day like an automaton: tidying up, preparing meals, washing up, pretending to read, pretending to watch the TV, smoking one cigarette after another, drinking shot-glass after shot-glass of whisky, all the while existing in a state of abject terror. What did I do to deserve this? I mean, I didn't do anything to that girl.

Why?

Maybe we'll never know.

To distract ourselves we find a small degree of solace in watching re-runs of Agatha Christie's *Poirot*. This is comfort food for the mind. The acting is good, production values high, and the locations excellent. They have managed to find a number of Art Deco buildings which have been fortunate enough to escape the wrecking ball. We should visit some of these places, I say to my wife. For her part, a lover of detective novels, she is remarkably adept in working out whodunnit, usually by the second ad break.[6]

Christie has a number of tried and tested plot devices, she explains; the doctor did it, the butler did it, the detective did it, and so on. You just have to work out which one she is using in this episode. Another programme we find ourselves attracted to is *Judge Judy*. Some channels show several consecutive episodes in stacks, so we record them and watch them one after another, editing out the commercials, which would otherwise render them too maddening to endure. Watching Judy Sheindlin in action is witnessing an exercise in logic. She is incredibly skilful at teasing out the truth and brushing aside prevarication. "I'd be happy to have Judge Judy hear my case," I say to my wife and she agrees. Sheindlin is always fair, always impartial and can

---

6 Later that year we saw a production of *The Mousetrap* at our local theatre. She had correctly worked out the perp by the interval.

spot a lie in a heartbeat. And that's what my case is about: lies. But why has Florence lied? Could it have something to do with the fact that I was her father's doctor? Speculation as to her motive swirls in my head almost constantly. I will never meet her, never have a conversation with her; therefore any opinion I form about her and her motives must be based solely on what we might call 'the facts'. Florence has gone to the police and made a series of extremely serious allegations of a sexual nature against me. These allegations are false, each and every one of them. Am I therefore entitled to call them deliberate lies? It isn't as simple as that. Maybe she has reached a point where she sincerely believes the web of allegations she has woven. She might even pass the most sophisticated of lie-detector tests. In which case it is perhaps just as well for me that lie-detector results are not admissible in British courts. But this does nothing to address the fundamental questions: why she has included me in her allegations, and how did she form them in the first place? I have a nasty feeling I will never know. Perhaps she doesn't even know herself.

As for the other men, Florence must have her own reasons for accusing them. I suppose I will find out in the end, when their statements to the police are released to my defence team. Will they have confirmed a tenuous connection with Florence, as I did, or will they deny having any connection at all? Of course if they have given no-comment interviews I may not find out until the case comes to court. Giving a no-comment interview in court, I suspect, would be a bad move. At this time it is all pointless speculation, but I still find myself wondering, what is behind it all? Is it all part of Alexander Coxhead's 'scattergun approach'? At this moment I don't have the faintest clue. Other than Owen, I don't know any of them, and I am too consumed by my own problems too care very much. I know the allegations against me are false; I am as sure as it is possible to be that the same applies to Owen; therefore I strongly suspect the allegations against the others are also false. But as I said, I don't know them and cannot vouch for them.

Wait. What about the warning?

Ah yes. The warning.

In this climate, no one is safe. *You* are not safe. At any time, someone from your past, someone you hardly knew and may have forgotten altogether, may come forward with false allegations of historical sexual abuse. Against *you*. It may even be someone you have never met. Yet in the current climate these claims will be believed by the police and prosecuting authorities. You will be arrested, and the police will treat your protestations of innocence with scepticism. Your file will be passed to the Crown Prosecution Service, who in all likelihood will press charges and move forward to prosecuting you in the Crown Court. Many months of waiting will ensue while you are put through an emotional wringer, waiting to see if they drop the charges or proceed to trial. Your life will be put on hold, and when the 'facts' of the case are made public your reputation will be trashed, whether or not you are found guilty. Your friends will believe your protestations of innocence. Others will say "No smoke without fire". It could happen to anyone. It could happen to you. Tomorrow.

And the advice?

Yes, that too.

If you are ever interviewed under caution, having been placed under arrest and accused of a serious crime, don't be as fly as I was in answering all their questions to the best of your ability in the mistaken belief you are 'helping the police with their enquiries'. Far better you deny everything (if indeed you are innocent), give a prepared statement to that effect and from that point give a no comment interview. I am not saying I was poorly advised in my police interviews, but I am saying I would do it differently should anything like this happen to me again. I am of above average intelligence and experienced in debate. But that did not prevent the police leading me to make a number of naïve and frankly unwise comments that left me in a far worse position than if I had said nothing at all. We have already seen in my own police interview how skilful the police are in twisting people's words and catching them out in apparent contradictions.

In the next chapter it gets worse.

Chapter Five

Abortion isn't a lesser evil: it's a crime.
An absolute evil. – *Pope Francis*

We have moved forward to Tuesday the ninth of August 2016, twelve noon. A phone call from my solicitor. The police have asked me to come to the station again "To clarify certain issues". When I arrive I am placed under arrest again. Not handcuffed this time, though it is made clear to me that I am not free to leave. It quickly emerges I am not here to "clarify" anything. I am to here to answer a fresh allegation. Before the interview begins, my legal advisor, Mr Coxhead, the 'surfing solicitor', speaks to the police in private to make the declaration that I had told him just after the first interview, namely that I *had* been Ken D's doctor. Then he joins me in the interview room to let me know the details of this latest allegation, prior to the police coming in to begin their interrogation.

"This time she says her father brought her round to your house back in 1996, or 1997, she isn't sure, and you took her into the top room of your house where you performed an abortion on her."

"What? That's ridiculous! I don't even know how to *do* an abortion!"

"I agree, it's pretty far fetched. But like I said last time, it's all part of this girl's 'scattergun' approach. Hopefully even the police won't take it seriously this time. Mind you, you can never tell these days."

Alistair signals he is ready for the interview to begin, and the police officers, the same ones as before, take their seats. They switch on their tape recorder and video camera, just like last time.

DC Orford begins by passing a typed letter across the desk. I can see from the letter-heading it was written by me. It is the original letter I had written to Florence's mother following the disappearance of her ex-partner, Ken D. I read it, and, strangely, my first thought is, you know, this really is a pretty decent letter. It begins with my expressing my shock on hearing of his sudden disappearance, and ends with the words:

"As you know, Ken was more than a patient to me, he was a good friend. I'm sorry to say I have no idea where he is now. He never kept me apprised of his movements. If I hear anything at all, however, I promise you will be the first to know."

I was so busy at that time in my life, balancing my full-time work as a GP with my family life that Ken's disappearance didn't affect me very much. One minute he was on the scene, if only on the periphery of mine, then the next I knew he had cut all ties and vanished. A lot of us speculated as to his reasons, but nobody seemed to know anything. Thousands of people disappear every year, some to evade the law, others to flee the crushing responsibilities of family life. Some turn up again after a while; others bury themselves so deep they are never heard of again. But back to the here and now; the fact that I *was* his doctor is beyond question.

"So why didn't you say so the first time we asked you?"

I answer that this was a long time ago; that there were five thousand patients on our list; that GPs on average have ten thousand patient contacts a year, so it isn't *that* surprising. Ten thousand patients a year; twenty years: as the Americans say, you do the math. All I can think is, thank God Alistair Coxhead got it in first, before they had a chance to nail me. But the incident will scarcely create a favourable impression in the minds of the investigating officers.

"May I ask you a question at this point?"

"Yes, what is it?"

"Have you been able to find Ken?"

"We are not at liberty to discuss that I'm afraid. Now let's move on. OK Mr Glascoe, you were previously arrested in relation to the rape of Florence D, a female under the age of sixteen, and that since that time a further disclosure has been made."

"Yes."

"Has your solicitor told you what that allegation is?"

"Yes."

"Can you tell me anything about it?"

"It's completely false."

I was learning.

"Anything else you'd like to say?"

"No."

"Florence is saying the procedure took place when she was thirteen years old. On a Monday in November, 1996, she thinks. And she says it took place in the attic room of your house. So, did you know her at that time?"

"I'd lost touch with her by then. I used to see Ken in the surgery from time to time, but I don't think I've laid eyes on Florence since about 1993. It would be perfectly easy to confirm that my regular working pattern throughout my career as a GP, and certainly in 1996, is that I would have been working virtually all day, every Monday."

"What about holidays, time off and things like that?"

"Most unlikely. It was not the half-term holidays, when I might have been away, and November is usually very busy, and Monday is the busiest day of the week. That's why most GPs work all day Monday."

I went on to explain the details of my working day; how I would conduct a morning surgery, do the house-calls, then go home for lunch for an hour or so, then back to work for afternoon surgery. Not a lot of time to fit in an amateur termination of pregnancy.

This feels different from the first interview. Last time I was in a profound state of shock. This time I feel almost bullish. This time the accusation seems so outrageous, so ridiculous that surely no one could possibly believe it. Wrong. Clearly, as before, the investigating officers believe every word of it. They quiz me about my gynaecological experience. I admit that I was a senior house officer in obstetrics and gynaecology, though it was back in 1975.

"Have you ever performed an abortion yourself?"

"No. I was only there to assist."

"Assist? What does that mean?"

"Well, to observe. I didn't actually do anything."

"And how were these abortions carried out?"

Now I'm getting flustered, so much so I forget the details of the technique and find myself describing another procedure altogether, known as a D and C.[7]

"And when these abortions were performed, would the patient be sedated, or totally unconscious?"

"Fully anaesthetised, unconscious in other words."

"What do you know about drugs used to procure abortion?"

"Not a lot. I suppose you could look them up in a pharmacology textbook."

At this point my solicitor halts the interview and, once the police have turned the recorder off and left the room, he turns to me and says:

"What are you doing? You're helping them too much. You don't have to do their work for them. That thing about looking up the details in a textbook. What the hell did you tell them that for?"

I curse my naïveté. Here I am, 'helping the police with their enquiries' again, like a good middle-class boy, forgetting they are motivated, not by a desire to get to the truth, but to put me behind bars for as long as the law allows. Once again, and once again too late, I wonder why I haven't been advised to give a 'no comment' interview, giving one or perhaps more prepared statements in response to the police's questions. That would have avoided my getting into the aforementioned scrape, certainly. Maybe it is because juries, even though they are admonished not to do so, cannot help drawing a deleterious impression of a defendant who sits there and says nothing.

"Have you ever performed an abortion since then, in your life as a general practitioner?"

"No. Of course not. Why would I? When you can refer people to a hospital so easily?"

The Abortion Act of 1967 was designed to do away with 'back-street abortions', and indeed the act produced its intended effect: with so many easier ways to go about obtaining an abortion; through the NHS, or private charities such as the

---

7 Dilatation and curettage, where the cervix is dilated and the uterine lining scraped away. Actually all the terminations I saw were 'STOPs' (Suction Termination of Pregnancy) where a vacuum sucker is introduced into the womb to remove the 'products of conception'.

British Pregnancy Advisory Service, the back-street abortion is a thing of the past. Prior to 1967 it is estimated there were anything up to 100,000 illegal abortions every year in Britain. Hundreds of women died as a result. But very quickly after the new legislation came in, the figure fell away almost to zero.

Once again it is apparent the police aren't buying my story. I listen as they relay Florence's account of how I did it. It doesn't make sense. Drugs used to bring about abortion take one or two *days* to work, not hours; likewise, at this stage in pregnancy (she says she was around twenty weeks at the time), 'breaking the waters', as she describes it, using a hook usually takes as long or even longer. And that assumes I possessed the skills to perform this intricate technical task. Even if I did, why would I take such a stupid risk, *and in my own home?* The answer is clear on their faces: if I was a sadistic monster, drunk on my power as a doctor. Then it would make perfect sense.

Finally, the 'Officer In the Case', Detective Constable Cath Orford says this to me:

"I have been asked to ask you this: what did you do with the baby?"

I stare at her incredulously.

"What did I do with the baby? I didn't do anything with the baby. There was no baby. The events you describe *never took place.*"

There then follows a discussion of the decor and furnishing of my house. Florence gave them a remarkably detailed description, but as DC Orford goes through it it is clear that she is describing the house as she saw it in March 1993, when she visited our house accompanied by her father. I point out how the house would have looked very different in November 1996, after substantial redecorating work. Florence has got it wrong. I start wondering how I can prove that. My wife Liz certainly can; she was the one who did most of the decorating. But that might not help. Wives lie for their husbands routinely. It's only natural.

They return to Florence's description of the abortion I am said to have performed.

"Florence has told us you gave her some tablets and an injection, which made her feel 'out of it'. She says you then took some kind of hook and inserted it inside her. She started having contractions which were very painful, and then the baby was born, dead. She says it was a girl. What can you tell me about that?"

"These allegations are completely untrue. They did not happen in my house."

She gives me a look as if to say, yeah, right. Then the interview is over. I am 'de-arrested', as the saying goes, and released, after being reminded of my bail conditions. Once again my legal advisor gives me a lift home; once again I refrain from quizzing him as to why the 'no-comment' strategy was not deployed. It's a bit late now anyway.

That very afternoon I write a letter to a gynaecologist of my acquaintance, not a personal friend, but one with whom I had had a professional relationship in the past, give him the description of events I have been given and ask him to provide a commentary. Bless him, within a few days he has got back to me stating that in his opinion her account is:

"*Wholly implausible and bearing no relation to reality. Breaking the waters or the use of abortifacient drugs would not procure an abortion within a couple of hours. The absolute minimum time would be twenty-four hours, and more likely forty-eight or seventy-two.*"

His letter concludes:

"*It appears she may have been watching the TV series Call the Midwife or has seen the film Vera Drake.*"

It seems impossible anyone would take these claims seriously, especially as they have been produced *after* the initial tranche of allegations, when she learned we had denied all the charges. Yet I will soon learn that I am wrong. In time, this absurd and outrageous allegation will indeed be added to the list of charges I face.

Once again, the following week, I visit my solicitor, this time the boss, Mark Crowley, to discover to my horror that this latest charge is in fact the most serious I face, more serious even than child rape.

"Procuring an illegal abortion in a minor, child destruction[8]; this charge alone could carry a sentence of twenty years."

"But surely no one would believe such an outrageous story?"

---

8 bringing about the death of a foetus; not actually murder but in law close to it

But even as I am saying the words, I am reminded of the words of a philosophy don I once knew: "As soon as you use the word 'surely' you're losing the argument."

My solicitor continues:

"It's all a question of what they can persuade the jury to believe. We will need to employ the services of an expert witness to refute the claims. Oh, and that will cost about £3,000 for each day of testimony. And don't forget, the prosecution will produce their own witnesses to challenge yours."

"What about the letter I gave you?"

"The prosecution will say it is tainted, because of your previous relationship. We will need to use a completely independent expert; someone who doesn't know you. We will send your letter to them, of course, but don't think that will be the end of it."

Every time I see him I feel worse. I yearn for him to say "Don't worry, it's going to be OK", but he won't. He can't. He knows it is all down to a jury's decision, and they may be so overwhelmed with horror at the claims, feel such sympathy for a doubtless tearful and emotional Florence that they will feel bad if they acquit on all charges, which will imply they believe her to be a serial liar. Perhaps, in order to appease their consciences, they will convict on one or two 'specimen charges'. But that won't be enough for me, or any of the others. I have to be acquitted on *all* charges, complete exoneration. Anything else will see me jailed and bankrupt. But, I remind myself, they don't have to believe her, or me. They only need to have a reasonable doubt about her allegations and I, and the others, will be in the clear. "A high standard of proof is required." These words echo in my head again and again. It is all I have to hold on to. Just as I leave, my solicitor says:

"By the way, next time we will need to talk about arranging a finance package to fund your defence."

Money always matters. Perhaps never more so than now. My legal team has discreetly asked for an up-front payment of £3,000, just to keep things going. If I am ever charged, they can apply for legal aid, though, they explain, with the funds I have available it is bound to be rejected. But unless a claim is submitted, there will be no possibility of recovering any of my legal expenses should I be found not guilty. Until 2010, defendants found not guilty could reclaim *all* their expenses, legally aided or not. Then the coalition government, led by David Cameron, changed all that. Thanks Dave.

I understand the reasons behind the decision. In the nineteen-nineties it became fashionable for some solicitors to use the services of high-profile QCs to try even relatively trivial cases. Superstar barristers, able to charge five or even six figure fees would find themselves defending shoplifters, drunk-drivers and low-level fraudsters. They would then be remunerated their huge fees from the public purse. Something had to be done.

But in law, as in medicine, each case should be considered on its own individual merits; that is to say every case is unique. I think a fairer system would be to allow judges to consider *full* reimbursement of costs on a case-by-case basis. It shouldn't be too hard to work out which cases are the deserving ones, principally those where the defendant faces a lengthy prison sentence, say, more than five years if found guilty. Defendants could be means-tested, requiring millionaires to fund themselves entirely, allowing others of more limited means to recover their full costs.

Now even if found not guilty I will only be able to recover a small fraction of my costs. I have already forked out three grand to my solicitor and we haven't even spoken to a barrister yet. Once that starts my bank account will start haemorrhaging money. Not that anyone would care about this very much. The public sees doctors as wealthy people, and to be fair, compared to the majority of the population they are. But I think it is worth pointing out that false allegations constitute a double disaster: to the reputation *and* to the bank balance.

When I retired from my job as an NHS GP in 2011 I received a substantial lump sum, along with a healthy pension. Only fair, I felt, as I had been contributing nine-and-a-half per cent of my income to my pension pot since 1974. Since my retirement I have often thought about what I might do with that money: buy a place in France perhaps, or a larger house here. Or simply keep it for a rainy day. Well, it's started raining now, and before long it's going to be coming down in torrents. My friend Owen has few savings and only a modest pension: he *is* eligible for legal aid. By the time the trial is over, we will be in almost the same position, because most of my savings will be gone. The only difference is the pension. That, at least, is secure. One of the first things I checked after I was arrested was whether my pension would continue to be paid even if I went to prison. The answer: yes, even if I were convicted of mass murder. Even Harold Shipman received his NHS pension in prison, and committed suicide the day before his sixtieth birthday in order to maximise his wife's widow's pension. As far as I am concerned, however, I think it is fair to say there is a lot riding on this.

*

I am a minor official in a church; a verger perhaps, or a deacon. To enter my rooms I have to walk through the nave. There is a service in progress; people are in prayer. Once aware of me one or two of them stop what they are doing and glance up at me. I am aware of a rumbling of discontent. One of the female parishioners hisses to her neighbour:

"Look! It's that doctor."

"Which doctor is that?"

"You know, the abortionist."

"Well if he's staying I'm leaving. Let's go!"

They get up and leave and others follow. Puzzled by this odd behaviour, I make my way through to my rooms. As I approach the door I hear the sound of murmuring, and as I enter I find a large number of people in there, including my wife. Other than her, they are not known to me. Their attention seems to be focussed on something in one corner of the room. I say to my wife, "Go and see what they're looking at."

She walks reluctantly to the corner of the room and looks down. She lets out a terrible scream and throws herself on the floor, weeping piteously. When the other people in the room notice my presence the murmuring ceases. One man turns to me and says:

"Ah, Glascoe, I'm glad you're here. Come gentlemen, let him pass."

I go over to the dimly lit corner and there, lying in a small black-painted crib, its white skin pock-marked with black and green blotches like decaying bread, is a dead baby. I start to scream.

Lying beside me, Liz starts and shakes me.

"Steve, wake up, you're dreaming!"

"Oh God."

"What was it about?"

"Oh, nothing really. I can't remember now."

But I *can* remember. In fact I don't think I'll ever forget.

Chapter Six

If you gaze long into an abyss, the abyss gazes into you.
– Nietzsche, Thus Spoke Zarathustra

Monday, the third of July 2017, eight am. 'The present day'.

I have just returned home from dropping off my wife Liz at Cardiff airport. In an hour she will board a connecting flight to Charles de Gaulle airport in Paris, where she will catch a non-stop flight to Narita airport, some forty kilometres outside Tokyo. On her arrival, doubtless jet-lagged, she will take a bus to Tsukuba, "City of Technology", about an hour's ride distant. There she will join with over two thousand of her professional colleagues from around the world, and on Thursday will deliver her own keynote speech, ironically, on the subject of 'Encouraging emotional resilience through psychotherapy'. I won't say she doesn't prepare well, though I will say she spent most of yesterday brushing it up, in particular reading it out loud, in order to make sure she can read it in her allotted time of eighteen minutes.

*

As I wait for Liz to return from that distant land, there is all the time in the world to cast my mind back over the events of the previous year, and commit pen to paper. It seems paradoxical to say that writing about my problems provides a welcome distraction from them, and I don't really understand it myself. But it works.

I am recalling a day in August of 2016; it doesn't really matter which one. They were the same, one after another. It was as if I was floating on a sea of fear. I found myself increasingly thinking about suicide. Doctors are very good at ending their lives. They may enjoy varying success at preserving life, but they know exactly what it takes to snuff it out. I have selected my method. A large knife through the heart. I know exactly where to place the blade: on the left side, between the fifth and sixth ribs, in a line straight down from the clavicle, or collar bone. This is the position of what doctors call "the apex beat", where the heart may be felt to beat most strongly. Death will not be instantaneous; it rarely is. A friend of mine, also a doctor, a cardiologist as it happens, committed suicide in this way. He went downstairs late one night, leaving his wife in bed upstairs. He selected their largest carving knife and plunged it deep into his chest. He did not die where he stood. He managed to walk outside his house and make it about thirty yards down the road before he collapsed. On hearing the front door open his wife woke up and went down into the kitchen. She saw the cutlery drawer open, and when she looked in she saw it was full of blood. Then she saw the blood trail on the floor and followed it outside. She found him collapsed on the pavement, his blood running into the gutter. She had no idea why he had committed this terrible act:

"He wasn't even depressed, not as far as I knew, anyway."

Coroners refuse to believe anyone can take their life for sound reasons. "While the balance of the mind was disturbed" is their mantra in almost every situation. They go to great efforts to avoid calling it suicide, presumably to spare the feelings of the family, though that must have been difficult in my friend's case. The reality is that there is a whole variety of reasons why people may legitimately decide to end their lives: long-term depression which has defied all attempts at treatment, terminal cancer, motor neurone disease; the list is long. In my case, it would be the prospect of spending the rest of my life in prison for crimes I did not commit. A man reviled across the nation and even around the world; who will need to be isolated from his fellow inmates even in a prison which specialises in sex offenders, lest someone take out their anger at him by slitting his throat or setting him on fire.

There is a widespread belief that people who take their own lives are cowards. People say: "They took the easy way out". I have never accepted this. To me, suicide is an extremely courageous act.

It is said that it is impossible for a conscious human being to conceive of the end of consciousness. That may be true, but when we try, we don't like it very much. Eternal blackness, an enormous empty void, that sort of thing. Therefore I contend that anyone who contemplates such a thing and then willingly embraces it must almost by definition be brave. I am not brave. I will not kill myself. I do not possess the courage. So I sat there, contemplating my possible future, feeling more wretched than I had ever felt before.

I was trying to read, Zola's *The Ladies' Paradise* as it happens. I was racing through it in late June; even though it was written in the 1880s it reads almost like a contemporary thriller. But then I was arrested and now I would read one sentence, then another and have to stop, put the book down and stare out of the window, and think Why? Why me? And what if she is believed? I'll be fucked. I would pick up my book again and read a few more sentences. Then stop. So it continued. I abandoned the book and went for a walk. Normally, received wisdom has it, a walk helps clear the head. Not today. I was hardly able to put one foot in front of another. My legs felt so heavy it was exhausting after only a few steps. The same thoughts swirled through my head constantly. I walked two miles; it felt like ten. At one point a pretty girl passed me. I dropped my gaze to the ground. It wouldn't do to be seen staring at a young woman. What if someone made a complaint of lewd behaviour? That would pretty much seal my fate at this point. I mustn't even look at a woman, still less a child.

I came home, turned on the television. I paid no attention to the programme. The thoughts continued to swirl. I stared at the carpet as though I'd never seen it before. Liz noticed what I was doing and attempted to comfort me.

"Steve. You're doing that thing again."

"What?"

"You're looking the carpet as though it was the most interesting thing you've seen in your life."

"Was I? I hadn't noticed."

"Well, you were. Look. You're going to be fine. Remember what your lawyer said. Juries are reluctant to convict on uncorroborated testimony, high standard of proof required. There is no way they can prove anything to beyond a reasonable doubt. Trust me. You're going to be OK."

I felt a little better. For a few minutes. Then the thoughts returned. Eventually tiredness took hold. I went to bed, fell asleep quickly, but woke at two am. The thoughts again. At two o'clock in the morning, *everything* looks bad. In normal times I have a technique for dealing with issues that trouble me in the middle of the night. It goes something like this:

Look. Is there anything you can do about this now? If yes, get up and do it. If not, shut up and go to sleep.

OK. Got it.

But this was *not* a normal time.

★

In some ways I am a fortunate man. It seems I am incapable of feeling down indefinitely. As the summer of 2016 progressed, slowly, painfully, I climbed out of the pit. I began to feel better. Then I was re-arrested and the charge of illegal abortion and child destruction was put to me. Down I went again. This is unendurable! I began contemplating suicide again. Another method occurred to me: travel to the Severn Bridge (the first one; its deck is higher than the second crossing), park at the motorway services, walk to the middle and jump off. Or dive. Naturally I would die, hopefully very quickly though not instantaneously. That hardly ever happens. But hitting the water from one hundred and fifty feet up is like landing on concrete. The neck snaps, the head cracks open like a melon; sometimes limbs are torn off. Death will come swiftly. But not instantly. Would I do it? Of course not. I am a coward. And what if somehow I did summon the courage? People would only say he must have been guilty, only the guilty do that. Not that I would care. I'd be beyond caring. But what of Liz? She would have to live with the stigma for the rest of her life.

"There she goes, poor thing. And to think, she never suspected a thing."

"Or did she? Come on, she must have known."

Rose West said she knew nothing of husband Fred's murderous activities. No one believed her. No one, absolutely *no one* will believe I committed suicide to escape from the hell I currently inhabit. There is only one solution to this: I must face my accuser, discredit her account and clear my name. Slowly I climbed out of the pit again, perhaps a little quicker this time. There is a learning curve. No one will believe this outrageous story. Will they? It hardly seems possible. But the police seem to have no problem believing it. DC Cath Orford, my would-be nemesis, she believes it all right. Every word of it. But then, it's in her job description.

That is why the police have bought into Florence's fantastical tales wholesale. The admonition to believe complainants has come right from the top. My lawyers' job will be make sure the jury doesn't.

*

In my mind the date has moved forward to Tuesday, the third of October 2016. It is three pm. My bail date.

As I am on my way to Cardiff Bay police station, I receive a call from my friend Owen.

"What the hell are you doing Owen? You know we're not allowed to speak to each other."

"I don't know what it said on your bail conditions, but in mine your name wasn't mentioned."

"What?"

This cannot be. How can he be on my list of people I am barred from contacting, yet I am not on his? It doesn't make sense.

"Look, tell you what. If your name isn't on my list this time, I'll call you later today. If I don't call, you'll know what happened."

My mobile phone is returned, which is not much help because I had to buy a new one anyway. Then to my solicitor's fury, I am re-bailed for a further four months, while the police 'pursue their investigations'. His protests fall on deaf ears. The deed is done. My bail conditions remain the same as before:

Not to contact the complainant, her mother, brother, or sister, directly or indirectly, in any way, "including electronically".

Not to have any unsupervised contact with anyone under the age of eighteen.

Not to contact my co-accused, directly or indirectly, in any way. And yes, Owen's name *is* on the list. No call is made to him today, nor will it be for many months to come.

★

Some time in August I receive a call from an eminent Welsh painter who was my patient for many years before the relationship slowly developed into a real friendship. After checking to find out how I was holding up, he asks:

"So, Steve, have you worked out why she made all these terrible allegations against you?"

A little shiver of fear runs through me, knotting my stomach. Is he going to be one of the 'no smoke without fire' brigade? Surely not. That is ridiculous. I calm myself.

"No, not really."

"I don't believe it Steve. Are you really so naïve as that?"

"I don't follow you."

"Come on Steve. It's about the money. These cases nearly always are."

"I'm sorry mate, but I can't believe anyone could do something like this for money. That they'd really be prepared to put five people in jail just to get some ready cash."

"Like I said Steve, your naïveté is touching. I looked it up on the web the other day, and complainants of multiple sex crimes stand to make up to twenty grand, even if the case doesn't go to court."

This is stunning news. I cannot take it in. I just mumble something about having a lot to learn, thank him for his information. We talk a little more but my mind is not on it. I keep thinking:

This is about money? Could it that simple?

This wonderful man has long been a friend, and has now proved to be one of my staunchest allies. He will continue to call every month or so to receive an update, always supportive, always injecting a note of hard reality. Thank God for him, and his like, of whom there are several. These people, their value is beyond gold, though one has to be in a situation of great jeopardy before this becomes apparent. In some ways I am a most fortunate man.

Chapter Seven

Il faut faire quelque chose
– Rene Magritte

The present day. Tuesday, the fourth of July, 2017. Ten am. The flying ants have arrived early. Not in their full flush of maturity, when they fill the air and send the swifts into raptures of feeding, twisting their necks in all manner of improbable angles to pluck them out of the air. No, these are youngsters embarking on practice runs, an advance party getting ready for the big day. I disturbed them when sweeping our front path, stirring them into a flurry of activity.

I am home alone, still waiting for Liz to return from her Japanese adventure on the eighth of the month, but the ants are waiting for the seventeenth. That day, I have noticed, is when they are most likely to take to the air in their millions, searching desperately for a mate before they lose their wings and die. Why the seventeenth of July? Statistics suggest that the nineteenth of July is the warmest day of the year in Britain, just as the nineteenth of January is the coldest. Of course that is only an average; the actual date will vary widely. But the ants in my garden seem to favour the seventeenth for their annual mating ritual. And they know what they're doing. Ants are some of the most successful life forms ever to appear on planet Earth. They've hardly changed since the time of the dinosaurs because they haven't needed to. They are perfect.

Homo sapiens, 'Wise Man', on the other hand, is very much an early prototype. A work in progress you might say. We have made some impressive strides; building great cities, travelling to the Moon, creating sublime works of art and so on. To the best of our knowledge, the human brain is the most complex structure in the Universe. Despite that we remain driven by deeply ingrained, primordial emotions: greed, jealousy, envy and hatred. And in some, the desire to dominate and degrade those weaker than ourselves. These may have been survival factors when we were hunter-gatherers; unfortunately they continue to blight the lives of human beings to this day.

Men have been taking advantage of women and children since the days of *Cro-Magnon*. Forgive me if this sounds like an oversimplification, but men are ten per cent bigger and stronger than women, and if necessary we can shoulder them aside for food. This is how the exploitation of women began. And for the same reason, exploiting children has been even easier.

When I was at medical school nearly forty years ago, I learned that incest occurs in anything up to twenty-five per cent of families, and is almost the norm in some communities. I remember finding that almost impossible to believe at the time, perhaps because I had been fortunate enough to have had an abuse-free childhood.

Later it emerged that the abuse of children was endemic in many institutions too: care homes, boarding schools, sports clubs, convents, in the Catholic priesthood; the list is long and deeply shaming. Slowly we have come to understand the devastating effects of abuse: eating disorders, cutting, drug addiction, long-standing depression, attempted suicide and suicide itself. Child abuse, once deemed to be more or less normal[9] has been considered a serious crime for many years. But for so long it was kept hidden, even by the authorities, who were reluctant to stir the hornet's nest of exposing cases to public scrutiny. Eventually things began to change. Scandals within churches of various denominations, previously kept carefully under wraps, became public knowledge. Then, with the death of Jimmy Savile a whole series of horrifying revelations about his obnoxious behaviour came to light. *Sir* Jimmy, the man who raised millions for charity, who was almost a permanent fixture on television with his appearances on *Jim'll Fix It* and *Top of the Pops*. To say he had become a great British institution, or even a national treasure, would not be overstating the case. But then, after he died, people who had worked with him for years and knew all about what sort

9 Samuel Pepys often indulged in activities we would now regard as child sexual abuse, yet it is clear from his diary it was accepted, albeit tacitly, at the time.

of man he was, went public with one ghastly story after another, each more terrible than the last. Why wasn't anything done at the time? was the cry from every quarter. Why indeed? He was *too powerful*, we were told. OK then, we said, but never again. From now on, no one would be above the law: not Stuart Hall, not Max Clifford, not even the much-loved Rolf Harris. One by one they were called to account and found themselves in prison, serving lengthy sentences for their crimes against children and young people.

It could be argued, however, that the change in climate of investigating allegations of rape began more than twenty years earlier. In 1982 the acclaimed documentary film maker Roger Graef made a series of films about the workings of Thames Valley Police, and when they were later shown on television the public was outraged. In one of them, a woman comes forward claiming she has been raped, and is taken to a cheerless interview room where she is quizzed by three detectives. In an appalling display of scepticism and hostility, they reject her claim out of hand.

Not long after the film was shown, the public outcry was such that the police instituted special 'rape suites', where a woman could feel more confident that her claims would be dealt with sympathetically, and in a more comforting and a supportive setting.

As I write, the balance has shifted almost entirely to believing the 'victim'. Alison Saunders, head of the Crown Prosecution Service, has set targets for the police and CPS to reach in bringing prosecutions for rape and historical sexual abuse to court. On one of my bail dates, I think it was in March, I asked the solicitor who was accompanying me on the day, Jonathan Webb, whether they really would go ahead and charge me.

"With the paucity of evidence, I don't see how they can. It would be such a stretch."

But stretch they did. They had targets to meet.

While rape and child sexual abuse remain common, fabricated claims of rape and historical sexual abuse are rare. But they are not unknown.

Jemma Beale had claimed up to ten men had abused her horribly over the course of four separate encounters. During one of them she said she was assaulted using barbed wire, though it later emerged she had injured herself deliberately to simulate the effects of this assault. She was believed by the police, by the CPS, and, most worryingly, by the jury. One man was sent to prison for seven years, serving two of them in the event.[10]

To give the police credit, they didn't leave it there. When a friend came forward to reveal Beale had confided in her, it was found she was a fantasist and attention seeker who was motivated by money.[11] But I don't want to find myself rotting in prison while the police work out there has been a miscarriage of justice. It needs to happen *now*. There are important differences between the allegations of Jemma Beale and Florence, but one crucial similarity: they're *made up*.[12] Not that Florence would concur with this assessment. I have no doubt she will insist to her dying day that her allegations are genuine.

To me the most worrying aspect of false allegations is that they damage the credibility of genuine complainants, and that, I suggest, is the biggest evil of all.

These are the thoughts concerning me today, which may be summarised as: will I see the flying ants next year, as they emerge from their caves under our patio and rise in their thousands into a balmy summer evening? Or will I be behind bars, disgraced and universally hated, most of my savings swallowed up by the lawyers and my house awarded to Florence by a civil court? Not that it will matter much in prison, of course. But what will I do there if the worst happens? I have begun to make some tentative plans:

<u>Smoking</u>. I am told smoking is shortly to be banned in prisons in England and Wales. As I am currently smoking well over two hundred cigarettes a week, this may be no bad thing. On the other hand, if I am going to end up dying in prison, what reason would I have to prolong my life? It is said that for every

---

10 In August 2017 Beale was sent to prison for ten years for perjury and attempting to pervert the course of justice; a more draconian sentence than many rapists receive.
11 She was awarded £11,000.
12 Towards the end of 2017, the entirely innocent Liam Allen was almost convicted of rape until last-minute revelations showed that his accuser too had been less than honest in her accusations.

year spent inside, two years may be subtracted from one's life span. At sixty-six, realistically, how long have I got?

Alcohol. I don't think that is permitted, though it is common knowledge that it is possible to obtain most mind altering substances, even in the most secure prisons. Which brings me to my next point.

Drugs. Weed, coke, ecstasy, benzodiazepines. Whether these will be available, and what the penalties are for being caught in possession of them I have no idea, and can only pray I never find out. But they might prove a much needed temporary escape from the endless drudge.

Reading. I have already devised a tentative reading list:

Zola. I have already read a few of the twenty books in Zola's *Rougon Macquart* series, but I could fill in the gaps, as well as re-reading the ones I have already completed. They would certainly stand a second look.

Balzac. His *Comédie Humaine* collection comprises no less than ninety-one works. I have already read *Old Goriot, Cousin Bette* and *Cousin Pons,* and if they're anything to go by I could do a lot worse than read the rest. And if I go down for the remainder of my life, which is by no means an exaggeration if found guilty on all counts, I shall have time to read the lot. If I can get hold of them.

Harry Potter. A few years ago I started reading *Harry Potter and the Philosopher's Stone* and put it down after three pages. It felt like a children's book, and not a particularly good one at that. But perhaps I have misjudged *la* Rowling. Dumbledore, Voldemort *et al* might provide an interesting contrast to the intricacies of the French masters.

Other activities.

Learn to play chess.

Play cards. Perhaps it is unrealistic to expect there to be a bridge school, though I can turn my hand to many other games: draughts, whist, poker, brag, gin rummy to name a few. And I could learn others. I have never learned to play cribbage, for example. Then there's dominoes. I've only dabbled in the past, but given time I could become a master.

Work in a garden. Prisons sometimes have gardens, don't they? Or maybe that's just something I saw in a movie.

Play snooker, pool, table tennis. Badminton? I'll admit I'm getting a little old for that one, or at least my knees are.

Juggle. Will they let me bring my juggling equipment? Or will I have to improvise?

Working out with weights. No. This cliché of prison life is an avenue closed off to me. I used to work a lot with hand weights, but as I entered my fifties I found my back would go after a few sessions. But I shall need some sort of activity to avoid running to fat. Just what, I'm not sure.

It's quite a list, but there could be an awful lot of time to fill. And there is one other thing I have not mentioned yet, which might just be my emotional salvation inside: I could write. I would, after all, be following in a noble tradition.

Chapter Eight

*Reading maketh a full man... but writing
maketh an exact man – Sir Francis Bacon*

Wednesday the fifth of July 2017. Alone for the first time in years, my wife still far from home, I am free to look back on the events of the previous year. And write.

I go back three seasons, to Thursday the fourth of October 2016, four pm. Two days ago, having been re-bailed for four months, I now face another lengthy period of limbo. I have abundant opportunity to pretend nothing ever happened and simply get on with my life. If I can.

In the stress management toolbox one of the most important tools is 'compartmentalisation': acknowledging there is a pressing issue, accepting there is nothing you can do about it now, and then, as the psychologists say, 'parking it'. This doesn't mean doing the ostrich thing; it's making a conscious decision not to allow it to play on your mind, and keeping yourself occupied with other things. Easier said than done. But you get better with practice.

As it happened, I had signed up for something sure to provide powerful distraction from the problems that beset me: I enrolled on the Master's course in Creative Writing at Cardiff University.

In May of this year, before any of this happened, I had gone to one of the 'Open Days' to find out more about the course. I was told straight away that I would need a university degree, a 2.1 or better.

"That's going to a be problem then."

"How so?"

"Well, I qualified in medicine, and they don't give firsts or seconds."

"I see."

"The thing is," I explained, "you can imagine the problems having first and second class doctors out there. Patients would only want to see the first class ones. And the second class guys would be sitting around with nothing to do."

"Yes, I can see how that might be a problem."

They then told me that probably wouldn't be an issue. Also that there was no formal interviewing process; you simply submitted a 6,000 word portfolio of your creative writing, and they made their decision on the basis of that material. In other words, your writing needed to be of a certain standard before you were even admitted to the course. Fortunately I already had plenty of material to choose from. I have been a strictly amateur writer since my teenage years, and following my retirement I had written several short stories, a few nonfiction pieces, and even a 35,000 word novella I had published on Kindle. Also I write a regular blog, naming after it after the early Christian heretic Pelagius, who was persecuted for claiming one could commune directly with God without the need of any priest to act as inter-mediary. In that sense he was an early advocate for free speech and individualism. A man close to my heart, in other words. I sent the university a selection of fiction and nonfiction pieces, and a couple of posts from my blog.

My portfolio was deemed adequate. I was admitted to the course. All I needed to do now was pay £6,500 (in three easy instalments) and turn up for the lectures. And write stuff.

Monday the eighteenth of September 2016, two pm. The first day of the Master's course. All the students and lecturers listened as the professor, Richard Gwyn, gave his 'induction' talk. He introduced his colleagues, and then invited us to intro-duce ourselves.

I sat and listened carefully as my eleven peers talked about themselves and explained their reasons for taking the course. It was immediately apparent I was the oldest course member by a considerable margin. At least half of them were fresh out of their undergraduate courses in English, that is to say they were no more than twenty-two years old. Hence I was not only old enough to be their father; I could have been their *grandfather*. I was older than all the lecturers too. Even the professor, acclaimed poet and novelist Richard Gwyn, was six years my junior.

Age was not the only thing that marked me out as different from the rest. There was, of course, another reason why I felt apart from the others. Just as someone who has spent a night of dissolution and hopes his colleagues will not notice, I was afraid they would somehow smell my fear, sense there was something dreadfully wrong in my life that could never speak its name. Perhaps I was worrying over nothing. But writers are known for their perceptive skills, are they not?

When it came to me, I said I was there to raise my writing skills to a higher level, adding:

"If I can produce one, just one, really outstanding short story as a result of this course it will have been worthwhile."

Quite understandably, everyone else on the course saw things very differently. For most of them it was a career move. They were just starting out in their professional lives. Several were writing novels they hoped would be published one day. We had a poet, a would-be television sitcom scriptwriter and two who were hoping to go on to be English teachers. A pretty diverse crew then.

It soon emerged that while everyone had already achieved a reasonable standard in their writing, there were no really outstanding performers (including me, unfortunately). I felt I was probably as good as any of them, except perhaps for a lad called Nathaniel. There was something special about Nat. He was in his mid to late twenties; slight of build with a strange, quiet intensity in his eyes. He was one of those students who didn't say much, and when he did it was in a voice so soft you had to strain to hear, but when he did speak it was always worth listening to. Nat had served as a paratrooper in Iraq and Afghanistan, and there was an atmosphere about him which suggested he had seen terrible things out there, things that had changed him. But he never talked about it and one didn't like to ask. His writing was sensitive and beautiful, although I thought his punctuation was appalling. The lecturers, however, didn't seem to have a problem with it, which was a bit of a shock. Clearly I had a lot to learn.

Unsurprisingly, I never told anyone about my problems. As I

saw it there was no point. I was still fostering the fantasy that somehow it would all work out fine; that when the CPS came to review the evidence against me and my co-accused, and found that it all revolved around the uncorroborated testimony of a single complainant, they would decide to take 'NFA' – 'No Further Action'. This was an example of what Orwell called 'Doublethink': believing two mutually contradictory things at the same time. My lawyer had already told me that the CPS probably *would* end up pressing charges, but part of me refused to believe it.

"But the whole thing is ridiculous!" I kept thinking. "Surely common sense is going to prevail at some point." Suffice it to say I believe I am the only person in Cardiff ever to go right through a one year, full-time MA course in Creative Writing (or perhaps *any* course) while being on police bail for serious allegations of historical sexual abuse. Without anybody knowing about it. True story.

What if someone found out? What if one of the students, a member of what is now known as the 'snowflake generation', somehow found out I had been accused of horrific crimes? They might be so outraged they would refuse to sit in the same room as me. Word would spread fast: soon the whole university would know and I would be suspended, as my remaining might damage the good standing of the institution. And even if I was cleared later, it might prove very difficult to be re-instated. But for the moment, everyone remained in the dark. For the moment.

*

At first glance the regime at 'Uni' (I will never get used to calling it that) seemed remarkably relaxed. Despite it being a one year, 'full-time' course, the timetable only encompassed one full day of lectures per week: Mondays between two and six pm, and Wednesdays between ten and one.

The rest of the time, presumably, was for writing.

The first term concentrated on the enigmatic issue of 'the Creative Process'. One by one, our lecturers took turns lunging deep into our subconscious minds, leaving seeds which, hopefully, would bear fruit in our creative writing. We were initiated into the legend of Orpheus and his journey into the Underworld, the concept of 'the Double' in literature and the inspirational value of 'Getting Lost'. In hindsight it was Richard Gwyn's lectures that lingered most strongly in the memory. Sometimes he would read a passage from a book in his slow, languorous style, say, *The Rings of Saturn* by W.G. Sebald, and let it hang there for long moments, waiting for us to absorb the significance of what we had just heard.

Was any of it working? I think it was. And I was in a position to know. Some of the most fascinating segments of the course were the workshopping sessions, where we could review each other's work. I can't begin to tell you how useful this was, even if it wasn't always good for the ego. To have eleven highly intelligent people tell you what was wrong with your beloved prose once a week could be a humbling experience. It can be very hurtful to have someone criticise your writing. It is a bit like having someone say something nasty about your adored baby, like "Ooh! He's sweet, but what's that ugly pimple on his nose?" Your first instinct is to punch them in the face. Students would often emerged bruised and battered from these sessions, figuratively speaking, even though we had been admonished to be gentle with our comments:

"Constructive criticism only, please. Try to be kind."

But one thing was evident: week by week, everyone's writing was improving.

Something else was becoming clear too: the apparently relaxed regime of the course was nothing of the kind. Producing one thousand five hundred words of new writing every week was actually quite demanding. And you couldn't just throw out a 'shitty first draft'. That was frowned on as being unfair to our fellow students. Not that people didn't do it sometimes, and it was immediately apparent when they did, though in a way you could hardly blame them. Apart from me, I think everyone else had jobs, some had two, and one had a young family to care for. I think I was the only one with nothing else to focus on other than the work. Well, I say nothing…

★

As a distraction from staring at the Damocles Sword hanging over my head, the MA course was the best thing that could have happened to me. For many hours every week I was so absorbed in it I almost forgot about my problems altogether. Almost.

On the one mile walk into campus, while reading or watching the television, while waiting for sleep to come, my thoughts continued to return to them again and again. I devised a quality measure when reading a book, listening to a piece of music, or watching a TV programme or movie. If they were sufficiently absorbing to keep me from thinking about my problems for more than twenty minutes, they were clearly very good indeed. Unfortunately, few came up to the mark. Channel 4's *Fargo* managed it, as did *Humans*. And, of course, *Frasier*. Watching Sidney Lumet's film *Twelve Angry Men*,[13] even for the fifth time, definitely qualified, as did Carol Reed's *The Third Man*, which I've probably seen even more often. Reading Nabokov's semi-autobiographical piece *Speak, Memory*[14] did the trick beautifully. One night we went to see Alice Ott perform Rachmaninoff's second piano concerto. That worked too. But the list was short, distressingly short, tiny islands of pleasure in an ocean of terror.

---

13 If I had Henry Fonda on my jury, I mused, I would be OK. But what are the odds of having someone like him?

14 It was on our recommended reading list, which comprised no less than sixty-seven books. By the end of the course I had managed about fifteen. But I had my own reading list too.

Chapter Nine

It is better to travel hopefully than to arrive
– Robert Louis Stevenson

The days drag on as I wait for Liz to come home from the Far East. Hours and hours of alone-time, more than enough to put pen to paper, and try to make sense of what has happened to me in the past year.

My recollections have moved forward to Monday the sixteenth of January 2017, nine am.

The new semester was about to begin. Christmas had come and gone. I hardly noticed. I was anxious to resume my studies on the MA course, mainly because I knew it would take my mind off my problems at least to some extent, but also because it would allow me to re-connect with my new friends who remained in complete ignorance of my situation. But how long would I be able to keep them in the dark? Perhaps there would be a press release, and then the whole world would know. As I walked to college on the first day of the spring semester, I tried desperately to put it out of my mind. And it was true, I was looking forward to seeing how my fellow students' writing was progressing.

Whereas several of my cohort were working on novels, I was putting in very different, self-contained pieces each week: a nonfiction piece about my favourite book, an essay about the possibility we might be alone in the Universe and the human race's terrifying responsibility in the face of that fact, and a short story about a man who awakes one morning to find his hands have disappeared.

People seemed to like my nonfiction the best, which in a way was disappointing. I so desperately wanted to produce a brilliant short story, one that might even win a prize one day, but so far it remained elusive. As for their writing, clearly at their age it might lack maturity, though there was no doubting they had talent and lots of good ideas.

But one thing did puzzle me: the absenteeism. There were twelve of us on the course, and although we were only required to attend lectures on Monday afternoons and Wednesday mornings, there was hardly ever a full house. The average was about eight, or two thirds, though occasionally there would only be three or four of us present. I was the goodie-two-shoes of the class: like the classic obsessional I am, I never missed a single lecture. But I was the only one with an unblemished record. All these people had handed over their £6,500; why weren't they making the most of their investment? One lad, our resident poet, was a keen hockey player and played for the university team. One of their practice sessions was on a Wednesday morning; I think you can guess which way he voted. One day a lecturer asked why he kept missing the Wednesday sessions and without thinking, I said:

"I think he's playing hockey."

There was a collective gasp from my peers, and I realised to my horror I had broken the first rule of student solidarity: never snitch on a comrade. I feared they might send me to Coventry, and had to do a lot of work apologising to everybody for my thoughtlessness, as well as letting the hockey guy know what had happened so he would at least be forewarned. Luckily I was forgiven. After all, the last time I was a student was forty years ago, and the *règle du jeu* had long been forgotten. But the truth is I wasn't *that* sorry. It was extremely annoying when people didn't show up. They were all very bright, and their comments, when they were present, were invariably useful. Hence their absenteeism deprived us of their insights, and this, for many of us, was almost the most important component of the course. From such a diverse group of students came a similarly diverse range of opinions, nearly all of them useful to budding writers. When people failed to show, I felt somehow cheated. The money paid to attend the course presumably meant even more to these young people than it did to me, with my comfortable pension: why then did they appear to feel so relaxed about not making the most of their investment?

*

Friday the seventh of July 2017, ten am. Something has jerked me out of my *recherche du mal temps perdu*: there is a little bubble in my vision today, and I am afraid. Everyone is familiar with floaters, those transparent, jointed little worms that appear before the eyes and move with the vision, particularly noticeable against a bright background. But this one is in the shape of an oval, and like a floater, it follows my gaze wherever it goes. It dances across the page when I read, just below the centre of my vision (if it were at the centre it would be intolerable, so I suppose I should be grateful for small mercies), and hovers uncertainly about the screen whenever I watch television.

Why am I afraid? Floaters, after all, are normal; simple clumps of cells which have desquamated from the lining of the retina, and float in the vitreous humour for a while before they finally dissolve. But this floater is different from anything I have had in the past, certainly more intrusive, and may be related in some way to the corneal transplant I had four years ago. And it is in my 'good' eye, my transplant eye. I've had floaters before; they hang around for a few hours, sometimes for days until I'm sure there must be a serious problem, only for them to disappear. I then forget about them until they recur, weeks later. Then I'm afraid again. Afraid my luck has run out, and that this is the first sign of my transplant beginning to fail.

As far back as 2009 I began to notice haloes appearing around bright lights. And while this may be normal under the influence of hallucinogens, they are anything but normal otherwise. I went to my optician, who diagnosed an unusual condition known as 'Fuchs' syndrome'. I'd never heard of it.

I learned that in Fuchs', the cornea loses its ability to drive fluid away from the front of the eye, which gradually becomes waterlogged. As it advances, the world is seen as if through a curtain of gauze. It is worst in the morning, but improves slowly during the course of the day. By late evening it has receded almost completely, but with morning it is as bad as ever. It is improved to some extent by the application of 5% salt water eyedrops, which by their osmotic effect drag fluid away. But the only real solution is a new cornea. My other eye is also affected, though less severely. It is a fact that concentrates the mind acutely; indeed, were I not distracted by other even larger problems at the present, it would be the biggest concern in my life.

I visit the eye clinic regularly for checkups. If I am sent to prison, I will probably continue to attend them, but handcuffed to a prison officer. They're strict about that sort of thing. Prisoners have been known to escape from hospitals in the past, so the authorities have to take precautions.

Every few minutes I wonder if my little fly has gone, then I notice it again. It is very odd. I have never experienced a floater like this before. I'm up at the eye clinic again in a couple of weeks; I should mention it to them. If I remember. I have a lot on my mind right now.

★

Last night I watched *2001: A Space Odyssey* on television, for the first time in many years. Throughout it I found tears coming to my eyes, so powerful was the sense of nostalgia it evoked. Despite its flaws I still consider it one of the greatest films ever made, and I will never forget the impact it had on me when I first saw it as an impressionable seventeen-year-old. Some lines from it persist in my mind to this day, like the immortal exchange where one of the crew members finds himself locked on the wrong side of an airlock:

"Open the pod bay doors, Hal."

"I'm sorry Dave. I'm afraid I can't do that."

When it came out in 1968 one reviewer said of it: "How to spend ten million dollars and confuse everybody." But as Stanley Kubrick's co-writer Arthur C. Clarke commented: "If you understood *2001* completely, we failed. We wanted to raise far more questions than we answered."

It certainly did *that*. The idea of artificial intelligence, previously the concern of sci-fi geeks and computer nerds, became a subject about which everyone had an opinion. In my case, the film sparked twin obsessions that remain with me to this day: when, if ever, will it be possible to build a computer sophisticated enough to simulate human thought,[15] and: come to that, is there intelligent life beyond the Earth?[16]

When I reached the final climactic scene, where a transformed Bowman contemplates the earth inside a shimmering ball of light, the tears rolled down my face. I let them stay there. But perhaps I am in a fragile state at the moment. My wife has been on the other side of the world all week, and I miss her badly. I need her right now; more than I have ever needed her before. But it will be all right soon. Tomorrow she will be home.

*

Saturday the eighth of July 2017, six pm.

"Tadaima! I'm home!"

Liz has that slightly shell-shocked look of someone who has sojourned in a distant and alien land, and just flown through eight time zones, traversing the North Pole *en route* in order make her way home. She seems halfway between eight pm, which it is here, and four o'clock tomorrow morning, which it is in Japan. Her clothes smell faintly of travel, as does her suitcase, in which the cats show considerable interest, climbing inside and sniffing it out thoroughly.

The delight at seeing me again shines in her eyes. Considering what she is returning to, I was worried it might not. When she has showered and settled down a little, I offer her a taste of home: a tin of spaghetti and mini-sausages on toast, topped with grated cheddar cheese. She gives me presents: two hundred Marlboro cigarettes, a bottle of Hibiki whisky (very expensive she says, "But you're worth it"), some Japanese sweets and a couple of very nice cotton tee-shirts.

Later, relaxing with a Rusty Nail, Liz offers her impressions of provincial Japan. It is a highly organised society, she says, regimented even, a place where smoking is not permitted in any kind of public space,[17] including outdoors (fine 1,000 yen, or

---

15 To date no computer has been able to pass the Turing Test, the industry guide for whether a computer is able to 'think'. And if you've had a chat with Alexa or Siri lately, you'll know they've still got a way to go.

16 Sadly, the consensus among the scientific community today appears to be: no.

17 though oddly, it is permitted in some hotel rooms, and even a few restaurants.

about £7), no graffiti anywhere (fine 2,000 yen), and no litter at all (fine 4,000 yen). She was struck by the excellent air quality, noticing the acrid odour of air pollution as soon as she landed in Cardiff, and also by how quiet the place was generally. No one eats on the street, wears ear phones or uses their phone in public. Conversation is carried on almost in whispers. The streets become deserted after nine pm, apparently even in large parts of Tokyo (though I cannot bring myself to believe the Ginza shuts down after nine). There is hardly any English or any language other than Japanese spoken, though some restaurants provide translations on their menus. She was particularly struck by one item: "Squid picked fish guts", though in the event she chose to pass on this delicacy.

As for the weather, skies were overcast throughout her stay, with high humidity and temperatures nudging into the thirties. She finishes her drink, fixes another for us both, and then makes this announcement:

"You know love, when this is all over and resolved in your favour, and provided you haven't smoked yourself to death by then, we're going to do Japan together, and properly this time. We'll go to Tokyo, and Kyoto; maybe we'll even climb to the top of Mount Fuji!"

Wow! What a girl!

I still don't know what we did to deserve her.

I tell her it is a brilliant idea, and then I relate how I had occupied my time with writing, watching stacked episodes of *Family Guy* and worrying about my Mum. My mother, ninety-three, lives in a pleasant little house on the coast in a little village called Ogmore-by-Sea. It is about twenty-five miles distant; a forty minute drive. Since the death of my father in 2004 she has lived there alone, but since 2009 has become increasingly afflicted by Alzheimer's disease. As it has progressed, we have deployed an increasingly comprehensive care package, and carers now visit her four times a day. I travel out there twice a week and take her for a walk on the beach, and my brother, who lives in Canterbury, comes down every month or so and stays for a few days.

Despite all this input, she is struggling to live alone. She often goes outside calling for her cat Daisy, and becomes distraught and tearful if she does not appear. This is most distressing for her neighbours, who often call me (and the social services) with updates of her behaviour. A couple of days ago I was called from her landline by two strangers she had invited into the house by waving to them from her front window. She had felt faint, I was told, needed to sit down suddenly and had gone a nasty colour. They, fearing she might have had a stroke, called an ambulance. I told them there was probably no need for that; she often felt faint when getting up quickly, owing to low blood pressure. She usually felt fine again in a few minutes, which had indeed happened on this occasion. The ambulance arrived quickly, and I spoke to the paramedic who, as it happened, was a former patient of mine.

"OK", I said. "So I don't have to give you my back story."

They gave her a cursory health check and, along with my reassurances, went away happy to leave her in the charge of her carer, who had arrived too. I expressed my gratitude to the two strangers she had invited into her home, but after I put the phone down I reflected on how fortunate she had been to attract the attention of two kindly, well-intentioned people. What if they had been unscrupulous, rifled her house and even beaten her black and blue in the process? Everyone is familiar with newspaper stories of elderly people attacked in their homes, with pictures of them languishing in their hospital beds, faces swollen and disfigured by cuts and bruises.

Liz and I agreed: Mum has reached a tipping point. For some months now we have been facing the grim possibility of having to place her in an old people's home, an idea that she has always resisted vigorously: "You're never going to put me in a home!" She invariably responds whenever the question has come up. "Leave my beautiful home and my wonderful sea view? Never!"

Unfortunately, it is now likely the social services will be forced to take a different view. But there is an alternative: a twenty-four hour, live-in carer. This would solve her problems, at least in the short term, and, as it turns out, may be cheaper than placing her in a home, as live-in care is funded to some degree by the social services. In a care home she would be responsible for the full cost. Mum has some savings, and is still in receipt of her late husband's pension. If it all works out, she may be able to stay at home for many months to come, until her savings run dry and she will have to go into residential care, and sell her house to finance it.

There is a platitude which goes: "God only gives you what he knows you can cope with". Nonsense. The random and chaotic nature of life ensures no such thing. Problems are piled upon problems with no regard to 'what we can cope with'. Though in this case, oddly, my mother's problems almost provide a welcome relief from the far more challenging issue facing me.

Chapter Ten

*Lying is an accursed vice... Once let the tongue acquire the habit of
lying and it is astonishing how impossible it is to give it up.*
– Michel de Montaigne, On Lying

The summer of 2017 wears on. Weeks to go before my final portfolio is due to be submitted; months to go before my Great Ordeal begins. Long days to look back over the dark days of last winter.

Tuesday January the thirty-first 2017, two pm. I am at Cardiff Bay police station, answering my bail. Just as they were prior to the first bail date last October, the days and weeks building up to this day have been a nightmare for us. I say us, because Liz has been through the meat-grinder along with me. True, she is not under the threat of a lengthy prison sentence, but should the worst happen, her life will turn upside down too.

My solicitor has been making a nuisance of himself, quizzing the police about how their investigation has been progressing. They handed their file over to the CPS some weeks ago, he was told. Maybe they have come to a decision about my case already; maybe not.

We arrive spot on time, but still have to wait, lightly sweating, for the customary thirty minutes before being called into the custody sergeant's office. This, I presume, is part of the softening-up process. Every minute that passes I feel a little more guilty, which I believe is the intention. I try not to let it show, force my face to adopt a cheerful *mien*. There is no mirror handy to check, but I doubt it is working. Liz has gone very pale.

Once inside his office, we learn that no, the CPS has not reached a decision yet. I am to be re-bailed for a further seven weeks, along with the other accused men, to allow them more time to consider our case.

"But this is ridiculous!" My solicitor fumes. "Either charge my client, or let him go!"

But the custody sergeant's hands are tied.

There is, however, a small change in the bail conditions. Hitherto, we have been barred from any unsupervised contact with anyone under the age of eighteen. This figure has been reduced to sixteen. We learn that one of the accused men has two children between those ages, and since July of last year he has been unable to spend any time alone with them; unable to take them out by himself, unable to be alone in the house with them, unable even to take them to school. It is for this reason the age has been changed. But Owen is still barred from baby-sitting his grandchildren.

Even the custody officer seems a little puzzled himself by the delays.

"I think I can say you will definitely get a decision next time."

"We'd like that in writing, if you don't mind."

"No problem."[18]

But we do learn something else. Amongst the sheaf of papers regarding the case, my solicitor notices the complainant must have originally gone to the police with her allegations some years ago. My solicitor is on them in a flash.

"Why the long delay between Florence making her original complaint and the accused being arrested?"

No explanation is offered. A police officer, for once, is giving a no-comment interview.

As we wait out the seven weeks before answering the bail date yet again we speculate about the mysterious delay between Florence's original allegations and our arrest. Could it be she fell pregnant not long afterwards, and felt she was unable to proceed with a trial at the time? Or, did the police and the CPS initially feel there was insufficient evidence to take a prosecution forward, but then, following the scandal over the Ian Watkins case, when the complainant was not believed to begin with, causing great embarrassment for the authorities down the line, decide to conduct a review of old cases and change their decision? My solicitor says there is no point speculating about

18 My lawyer never did get anything in writing.

this now, but that doesn't stop us doing it. It is very strange though, he admits that. But the truth, he assures us, will come out in the end.

Meanwhile the MA course goes on. The second semester concentrates more on the *teaching* of creative writing. It is one of the course's 'selling points'. And I have considered the possibility of teaching one day, at a night-class perhaps, or some other venue. Good God, I think, it might even be one of the things I do if I get sent down for a lengthy spell. Liz stamps on any speculation about what I might do in prison.

"It's not going to happen, so don't even go there."

It is doubtless good advice, but I can't help it. Though I do manage to keep it to myself for the most part.

The teaching component of the course is not as popular among the students as the sessions on the creative process. Absenteeism rises, though it is not as high as in the undergraduate course I sit in on as part of our training. Attendance rates there hover around thirty per cent. Once a student emailed the tutor explaining he would not be attending the next class because of 'lack of motivation', the clear implication being that it was somehow the tutor's fault. I kept thinking about my medical school days, when attendance rates never fell below ninety per cent. There you couldn't afford to miss anything for fear of falling behind. And the more you missed, the more difficult it would be to catch up. That's what I *call* motivation…

I did enjoy parts of the teaching course though. It enabled us to take several 'away days': to a junior school,[19] a college of further education, the Centre for Lifelong Learning and once, to the National Museum of Wales, where we were asked to select a painting and write about it for twenty minutes. I quickly made my way up to the wonderful Davies Collection on the first floor, where I walked among its treasures, waiting for one to catch my eye.[20] But teaching held little interest for most of the course

19 Thankfully, I was never placed in a position where I found myself in unsupervised contact with minors.

20 It didn't take me long to make my choice: Van Gogh's *Rain – Auvers*. Painted in August 1890, only a month before his inner demons drove him to take his own life, it shows a tiny village in the distance, with a vast, billowing cornfield occupying the foreground. All across it, great slashes of rain slant down onto the corn. It seems an appropriate image for Cardiff.

members. Like me, they were there to improve their writing, with a view to having their work published one day. And for me, it helped provide a timely diversion from the problems which would otherwise have dominated my every waking moment.

Chapter Eleven

Life is not a walk across a field
– Boris Pasternak, "Hamlet"

Tuesday, the twenty-seventh of February 2017, ten am. Eleven months to go before my trial is due to begin. Slowly, painfully, I am beginning to adjust to my new life. It is fair to say that human beings can get used to almost *anything*, even living with the prospect of spending the rest of one's life in prison for imaginary crimes. But however well integrated one might be psychologically, stress will always find a way to manifest itself. After the initial shock of my arrest wore off, I began to develop an alarming variety of physical ailments.

The first things to give trouble were my hips. Trying to move after even brief periods of inactivity would see me hobbling around, shuffling uncertainly, shoulders hunched, head down.[21] One day, while walking back from one of our numerous visits to my solicitor's office, my wife suddenly exclaimed:

"My God! What's wrong with you? You're walking like a two hundred year-old man!"

"Really? I hadn't noticed."

I arranged to have an X-ray and the report stated only "minor degenerative changes in keeping with the age of the patient". Great. So it wasn't the onset of advanced osteoarthritis of the hips, with a hip replacement or two not far down the road. It was good old-fashioned stress. And the aging process.

Then I caught a horrible cold, which with my emphysematous lungs turned almost immediately into a severe chest

---

21 Much later, I read online Sir Cliff Richard's impact statement regarding his action against the police and the BBC. He described almost the exact same thing happening to him after his homes were raided. He tried to play a little tennis with his coach, but had to stop after only a few strokes.

infection. It took two courses of antibiotics and a prolonged course of oral steroids to bring me through. I wasn't right for nearly two months.

It was perhaps no coincidence that just before I went down with my chest infection, word began to filter back to me that the police were tracking down my son's old school-friends, both male and female. Later we learned they went to great lengths to find as many of them as they could. One by one they were asked: did Seth ever report being mistreated by me? Sexually, or in any other way? Thankfully they were all quick to disabuse them of any such notion. But the very fact they had chosen to root them out was terribly disturbing.

Was there *anything* they wouldn't stoop to? To drag my dead son into this, it seemed despicable to me. But it did illustrate the lengths they were prepared to go to in order to take me down. It would be many months before the real reason for these interviews became clear.

Finally three weeks later, the last straw. A close friend visited and we had a long chat. Perhaps it was sitting in one position for a prolonged period of time; perhaps it was the dark nature of the conversation we had (we went through all the recent developments in my case), but not long after he left I noticed my back stiffening up. The following morning it was so locked I couldn't even get out of bed. Fortunately it occurred just as 'reading week' began at university;[22] otherwise there was no way I could have gone in, thereby spoiling my hitherto perfect attendance record.

It took me over twenty minutes to struggle out of bed to the toilet, and when I finally did, I found it too painful to stand over the bowl, or even sit on the seat. I made it back into the bedroom and announced to my wife:

"I don't know what to do. I can't even pee!"

At first she was terrified, thinking I meant I had gone into urinary retention, but when I explained the situation she came up with a solution:

"Look. Tell you what. You just stand there and have a fag. I'll

---

22 It is a well recognised phenomenon that stress related conditions often come on during periods of *decreased* stress. Migraine sufferers, for example, often experience their attacks on their week-ends off, or while away on holiday.

make a cup of coffee and let's see what happens."

Twenty minutes later I was able to relieve myself. I spent the rest of the day in bed, painfully trying different ways of arranging my body, but there was no position in which I could make myself comfortable. I started swallowing codeine tablets like smarties, something I very rarely do. Beyond rendering me constipated, they made scarcely any difference. I've had bad backs before; they've ruined a few holidays over the years, prevented me playing sports from time to time, but this was by far the worst I'd ever had.

Eventually, after some weeks, I started to improve. Liz gave me some yoga moves to practise, and the following week I went to a masseuse. I wasn't sure how much it achieved, if anything, but I was able to go back to 'Uni' on schedule, though still holding myself rather stiffly. If anyone noticed, they didn't say anything. After three weeks it had almost gone, though I continued to experience twinges from time to time, which put the fear of God into me. What if something like this happened during the trial? I could only hope it wouldn't.

Just when I was convincing myself nothing good was ever going to happen to me again, it did. Among the many people I wrote to asking for letters of support was my former general practice partner. In some ways it was a risky move. We had gone through an extremely unpleasant split in 2000, he taking the two other partners and nearly half of our patients with him to set up a new practice nearby. Partnership splits are like messy divorces; there is always a lot of bad feeling, which might be summarised by what I call the 'B.A.R. Syndrome': Bitterness, Anger and Resentment. I was half expecting him either to ignore my letter, or write back saying something like "I'm afraid I am not in a position to write any kind of supporting letter for you". I couldn't have been more wrong. Within a week he wrote back to me, stating he would be happy to testify in court on my behalf. I reproduce his letter verbatim:

"I knew Dr Glascoe well and worked with him closely throughout the period of time covered by the allegations against him. In all that time I never heard even the faintest suggestion of him behaving inappropriately towards women or children. Regarding the allegation

that he performed an illegal abortion, my opinion is that Dr. Glascoe possessed an average skill-set for a general practitioner, and simply did not have the skills to carry out such a procedure. He was known for his use of several types of alternative medicine in his practice, including homeopathy and acupuncture. He was a popular doctorn whose patients would often wait a long time to see him. He had a reputation for spending a lot of time with his patients, and even had the nickname of 'the patron saint of lost causes' for his work with homeless people and drug addicts. Finally I should add that our relationship ended in considerable acrimony in 2000 when our partnership split, and in no way would I consider him a friend."

It was an amazing letter. I've heard of being damned with faint praise, but this was being *vindicated* with faint praise. In his view I simply wasn't *skilful* enough to have performed an abortion, and this endorsement came from someone who was definitely *not* my friend. My solicitor considered it, along with the letter from the gynaecologist, as one of the most valuable letters of support I had received so far. The letter, as well as all the others, were later sent to the CPS for their consideration. Will they take any notice of them? We shouldn't have to wait long to find out. The time for my next bail date is approaching rapidly.

Chapter Twelve

Strike me dead – can't see the way,
It's lost we are, what can we do?
Could be a demon's leading us through fields
In circles, and we've gone astray.
– *Alexander Pushkin*

Friday the seventeenth of March 2017, 12.30 pm. The latest in my series of appearances at Cardiff Bay police station to answer my bail. Surely we will have an answer this time. Oh dear, there's that word *surely* again.

Here we are yet again. The waiting game. After the customary thirty minutes I am called into the custody sergeant's office for the third time since this whole process began. My wife sits outside. Only my lawyer may accompany me. The police officer says:

"The CPS has asked for bail to be extended for a further three weeks. Bail conditions will remain as before. Mr Glascoe,[23] sign here please. And here. And, here."

"I'm sorry, but I just cannot believe this. You assured my client last time there would be a charging decision today. Now this!"

"I'm sorry too sir. Unfortunately there's nothing I can do about it. But I can tell you the decision came from a high level. It has been signed off by the divisional commander, and he has been in touch with the Chief Constable himself about it."

"Look, I realise this is down to the CPS, but do you know *why* they haven't been able to reach a decision yet?"

"Off the record sir, I can tell you that the CPS haven't

---

23 From the outset the police, and the CPS, have always referred to me as Mr, rather than Doctor Glascoe. I'm not sure why. I'm not saying it is a problem, more something I registered.

actually *looked* at the case yet. They've been dealing with two complicated murder cases recently, and they haven't had time to examine the papers. And there is another reason why the bail has to be extended. We are dealing with a highly vulnerable complainant in this case, and we have been told there is a significant risk of her *dissolving* should the accused be released from bail."

For once even Mark Crowley seems lost for words.

We go outside and rejoin my wife. She is furious we will have to wait another three weeks, even more so when she learns the CPS haven't even opened the file on our case yet. But then she has always felt angrier about the whole thing than I have. Me, mostly I've just been afraid. We go home, back to limbo, back to pretending like nothing is wrong for another three weeks.

*

Thursday the sixth of April 2017, four pm. A phone call from my solicitor. The CPS have given him a heads-up: I *am* to be charged tomorrow.

"Oh God."

"I'm sorry, Stephen. I know this is very grim news. But you may recall I warned you this would probably happen when we first met to discuss your problems last July."

"I know, but..."

"Also, I need to warn you of the slim possibility you may be held on remand prior to your appearance at the magistrates' court, so you should bring an overnight bag containing your medications, your passport and some sort of proof that your mother has Alzheimer's and needs your support. It might be important."

I put the phone down and sit motionless for many minutes. My wife bursts into floods of angry tears.

"That bitch!" she yells.

"How could she do this to you? To us? And you didn't even do anything! All you did was be a friend. And a good friend. And now she's trying to destroy us! I hate her!"

Tears continue to roll down her face. It is frightening: I have never seen her like this before. And now the words tumble out of her in a furious, sobbing torrent.

"You know, when I was young I used to trust the police. Think they were the good guys. Boy, do I ever know different now. Now I wouldn't give them the steam off my piss. They aren't interested in justice; they're just interested in screwing you and the others because they've decided to believe every word that woman has told them. It's so unfair!"

"But you know how it is, they've been told to believe by the CPS."

"Yes, and that's even worse! We all know the police aren't too bright, but the CPS, they're lawyers, above average intelligence you would have thought. They're supposed to be the guardians of the people, dedicated to justice. But they're just as bad!"

What can I say? I cannot disagree with anything she has said; indeed I envy the uninhibited anger with which she has expressed it. But at this moment I am too paralysed with fear to show the rage which bubbles inside me. The time may come when I will be able to bring it out in the same way she has, but that time is not now. Fear, I have found, trumps every other emotion.

That evening I call a friend who has served as a magistrate in the past. She says that the possibility of my being held on remand is not at all remote.

"I'm sorry, Steve, but there's a very good chance of it."

I didn't think I could feel much worse than I do already, but I do.

One of the reasons we were charged at that time was because of a change in the bail regulations. Hitherto, bail could be extended almost indefinitely, and people could find themselves on bail for years. Now the limit has been reduced to just twenty-eight days. The accused must either be charged at that point, or released from bail. Pity this hadn't happened a little earlier; we might all have been saved a great deal of stress.

Friday the seventh of April 2017, eleven am. I have now been on police bail for just over nine months. It is now just under nine months to go before my trial, a trial which I now know *will* take place. On the advice of my solicitor, I have my passport with me, an overnight bag, and the letter about my mother. A number of friends have asked me how much my bail money is, but they've been watching too much American television. Police bail does not require any money to be handed over. After the standard thirty minute wait, I am invited through the combination-lock door into the custody sergeant's office.

It feels different today. For the first time since the original police interviews, lead investigating officer DC Cath Orford is present, standing behind the sergeant. Tall, slender, short dark hair framing her tight little face, she is wearing a long dress, dark red in colour. She makes no eye contact, fixing her gaze on a point somewhere near my left shoulder. Her expression is impossible to read, but I think that inside she must be feeling a sense of deep satisfaction at today's events. It begins.

"Mr Glascoe, you are today charged with seven offences. They are, that on unspecified dates between January 1st 1989 and December 12th 1997, you committed two offences of gross indecency and three of indecent assault against Florence D, a child under the age of sixteen. Further, that in the month of December 1997 you did rape Florence D, a child under the age of sixteen. And that in the month of November 1996, you did procure an abortion for Florence D, a child under the age of sixteen, by administering noxious substances and introducing an instrument to procure said abortion."

The only charge that appears to be absent is conspiracy, or 'joint enterprise'. With the attacks on her instigated by her father, the CPS appear to believe that all the accused acted individually when they abused Florence.

I almost miss the part where they say I am *not* to be remanded in custody and that they do not intend to seize my passport. When I do realise what was said I ask my solicitor to go out to my wife and tell her the 'good news'. A great pall of silence fills the room in his absence. When he returns I am about to say "Not Guilty", but my solicitor touches my arm. I am to say nothing at this point. DC Orford stands, motionless, like an awful avenging angel, her face impassive, eyes still fixed on an unspecified point. More words are said, but I have stopped listening. A sense of unreality, never far away during the last months, descends on me with unprecedented force.

They are going to press charges. Seven separate ones, each

one worse than the one before; everything in fact that Florence accused me of in the first place. They bought the whole package. I am stunned by the enormity of it all, part of me still unable to take it in.

It is all over very quickly. I am given a date to appear in the magistrate's court, and then released. It is all precisely as my solicitor predicted all those months ago, which seems like an age. But at least I am free. For the moment.

★

It is Tuesday, the ninth of May 2017, ten am. Cardiff Magistrates' Court. How accommodating of them! Not one of my dates with destiny have clashed with my study days at university, and soon the course will be over. I have informed most of my closer friends of recent developments, as well as my professor, Richard Gwyn, and my personal tutor. Given the almost inevitable publicity my case will attract, it seems only wise. Once again I have brought my little pack: passport, overnight bag and letter about my mother. None of these are needed in the event. And in a clever move, because there is no charge of 'joint enterprise', Mark Crowley has successfully petitioned for the removal of the bail condition about the co-accused not to contact each other. At last I will be able to speak to Owen.

The proceedings are over in minutes. The co-accused are asked to give their names and addresses, and the charges read. No plea is entered at this stage. That will happen later, at the Crown Court. That doesn't stop one of the accused, Simon C crying out "Not Guilty!" when the charges against him are read out. His face means nothing to me; neither do the faces of the E brothers. Between them they face a total of nineteen serious charges. Simon looks as if he might burst with barely suppressed rage; the brothers study the floor intently, their expressions blank.

Before we leave, my lawyer goes outside to see if there are any press waiting for us. Somewhat to his surprise, and certainly to mine, there are none. We walk home unmolested by photographers. But will the story appear in the newspapers? The answer, to my astonishment, is no. So I needn't have told all those people after all! And I have a few more months of anonymity before my name becomes public property. My mind cannot resist speculating what might have been tomorrow's headlines:

"CARDIFF GP CHARGED WITH MULTIPLE SEX CRIMES"

I have been incredibly lucky this time. But it is only a question of time. Soon it will happen. And even a headline like this pales in comparison with the ones that may be awaiting me next year.

I didn't see Owen in court; he is due to appear later this afternoon. I ring him, and it is his turn to be shocked that I have contacted him. I explain why it is all right to talk to each other now, and invite him to come over to my house after his appearance before the magistrates. It is an emotional reunion after so many months, but so beautiful. To be denied the right to speak to one's closest friend for so long has been one of the worst aspects of this case. Now, at least, that restriction has been lifted.

Seeing him for the first time in many months, my first thought is that, other than an understandable pallor, he almost looks like his old self. His wife, however, is another matter: poor thing, she looks awful. But how must *I* look? Friends tell me I don't look too bad, *considering*. But that qualifier speaks volumes.

As we catch up, I learn he faces only two charges, one of gross indecency and one of indecent assault. Facing a tariff of only eight years, he is in nothing like as much trouble as I am. But it is bad enough. To my horror he admits he did not have a solicitor with him at his interview. Sure he is innocent, sure he has nothing to hide, but to talk to the police without a lawyer present is insanity.[24] Owen is an intelligent man, but here he concedes he made a grievous error. Moreover, he compounded his error by not seeking any legal advice until after he was formally charged. Without a solicitor to disabuse him of such a

---

24 Legal advice in these situations is always free of charge, so there really is no reason why anyone should not take advantage of a lawyer's help.

notion, he convinced himself that the allegations would never amount to anything. And for the same reason, apart from his wife, he has told no one of his problems, no one. I tell him how valuable my friends have been since my arrest; how many of them have provided letters of support. He tells me he has been bombarding DC Orford with emails protesting the injustice to which he and the other accused have been subjected; indeed, he has fired so many in her direction she has written to his solicitor complaining of "harassment", and demanding he desist. He has complied, albeit reluctantly, but we are agreed that he has clearly got to her, which can only be a good thing.

One of the subjects he has pressed her about is a photograph the police claimed to have in their possession. The police had told Owen they had been given a picture by Florence which was highly compromising. According to them, the picture, apparently taken at one of my parties, shows Owen lying half on top of a young Florence. Clearly such a picture would take some explaining. Owen asked if he could see it. One of the police officers actually reached towards a big file box that lay on the floor beside the desk, but his hand was stayed by Cath Orford, who said something like "You'll have a chance to see it in good time". Owen has repeatedly demanded to see this picture, but so far his demands have fallen on deaf ears. In the event the photograph was never produced in any of the subsequent disclosures. Florence insists the image does exist, but has been unable to find it. There is no doubt in my mind, however: no such photograph was ever taken.

He tells me has become involved with several groups campaigning for justice for the falsely accused, and uncovered a few cases even more horrific than our own. There are cases, he tells me, of men spending lengthy terms in prison having been accused by a single complainant, those accusations being believed wholesale by the jury. I congratulate him for finding such an effective coping mechanism, because he says his work with these groups has, as writing has in my case, helped him to cope with his predicament. But his stories of many falsely accused, completely innocent men finding themselves in prison sends my morale slumping to a new low.

I am almost relieved when eventually he and his wife leave. In the coming weeks we will speak on the phone and email constantly, making up for lost time, but I will tell him I don't find his horror stories helpful, and ask him to keep them to himself from now on.

Tuesday the twenty-third of May 2017 eight am. I have been listening to the BBC's *Today* programme since my teenage years, though since July of last year I have put it on solely through habit and in reality pay scant attention to the content. I have been far too consumed by my own problems to listen closely to the news, but this morning something penetrated. Last night a suicide bomber blew himself up amid the crowds leaving a pop concert in Manchester. Twenty-two people lost their lives; hundreds more were badly injured. Islamic State was quick to acknowledge the bomber as one of its foot soldiers. As someone who has lost a child my heart goes out to the bereaved who must spend the remainder of their lives coming to terms with their loss. And in my current emotional state I find myself reliving this agony more acutely than ever.

*

The Crown Court date is set for the sixth of June, but this is delayed at the request of the CPS, first to the ninth, and then to the sixteenth of the month. On the eighth of June, the nation looks on agog as Theresa May is returned to office, if not power, nursing a significantly reduced majority. When Norman Lamont coined this phrase referring to John Major in the 1990s, it was just a spiteful piece of *schadenfreude*. This time it is the literal truth. And Jeremy Corbyn, previously felt to be an impediment to victory even by many in his own party, is suddenly seen as an asset rather than a liability. Meanwhile, Boris sits it out at Chevening, biding his time, still dreaming of the Iron Throne. Strange days indeed.

Saturday the tenth of June 2017, eleven am. A huge document comprising over one thousand five hundred pages is forwarded to me by my solicitor. On page one is embossed the Royal Coat of Arms, noble escutcheon supported by Lion and Unicorn, around which are entwined the famous mottos:

DIEU ET MON DROIT

HONI SOIT QUI MAL Y PENSE

Followed by the words

REGINA VS STEPHEN GLASCOE

Regina! My God! The entire panoply of the State is ranged against me, from Her Majesty the Queen on down. What hope do I have? It is true I have been expecting this; nonetheless just seeing the word in print fills me with an awful sense of foreboding. It takes some time to gather myself, take a deep breath and read on.

It contains the police interviews of the accused men, a series of witness statements from friends, teachers and counsellors to whom Florence has related her tales of abuse, and transcripts of the no less than sixteen interviews given by Florence herself. It is impressively titled *'Operation Violet Oak'*.[25] I find myself thinking, how did they come up with *that* name? And, wow, we've had a whole police operation named for us! More importantly, I note that I stand at number one on the list of indictments: of the five accused, I face the most serious charges by a considerable margin.

The witnesses include two teachers, neither of whom recall much of their encounters with the complainant. It is hard to see how they will be of any evidentiary value.

Other statements come from friends she made through various 'survivors of abuse' websites.

There is a long statement from her psychotherapist, with whom she clearly enjoyed an unusually close and, some might say, unconventional professional relationship.

But the meat of the document, nearly eight hundred pages of it, is taken up with transcripts of the interviews Florence gave to the police, dating from January 2013, through June and July 2016, and closing with a particularly lengthy interview conducted at the end of October last year. I hardly warrant a

---

25 I have searched extensively for any reference, anywhere, to a 'violet oak'. There are over six hundred varieties of oak tree around the world; not one has the prefix 'violet'. It seems somehow apt: an imaginary name for the investigation of an imaginary crime.

mention until the fifth interview, but then they become gradually more detailed and horrific in their accusations of myself and others.

It is not until October 2016, when Florence learns that her psychotherapist's notes are being sought by the police that she goes back to them and launches her final round of allegations against me, and, if such a thing were possible, they are the most disgraceful of all.

She has already accused me of stripping her naked and leering at her, of digitally penetrating her, forcing her to masturbate me, of performing an abortion on her against her will and then, the following year, raping her. Now she accuses me of being part of a child torture ring involving at least four children, including my own son, who was only one year old when these sessions began, and two 'blonde haired girls'. Although the sessions allegedly spanned several years, she never discovered their names.

Of these children, my son is dead, while the two 'blonde-haired girls' remain unidentified. Hardly an impressive list of witnesses.

I ought to be horrified by these scurrilous allegations, but actually I find them almost laughable. This is crazy stuff. Surely no one is going to take them seriously. But there's that word 'surely' again.

But I am wrong. When the list of charges are sent to my solicitor shortly before my appearance at the Crown Court, there are eight new ones added to the original set of seven. All of them refer to these alleged episodes of child torture, or 'inducing a minor to commit acts of gross indecency', as the prosecution refers to them. Clearly the CPS believe these allegations, as they do all the other fantastical claims she has made against me. And I am Number One on the indictment, now facing a tariff of twenty-five years or more. Time to find me a good barrister. But before I do there is another problem to negotiate; not one that threatens my freedom or my bank balance, but one which threatens to destroy my oldest friendship.

Within days of receiving the various witness statements from the CPS, Owen is on the phone and not best pleased.

"Why did you tell the police I went to those parties? I never went to any of them. What the hell were you playing at?"

"Look, calm down. I said I wasn't sure; it was a long time ago, that you *might* have been at one or two."

"Well you've got to put it right. Now think hard. Did you see me at any of those parties?"

"No, I don't think so."

"Right then. In that case you need to go back to them and tell them what you've just told me. Do you realise how much shit you've landed me in?"

"OK, I'll check with my solicitor and if he thinks it's appropriate I'll get right on it. But while we're on the subject of major league cock-ups, what about what you said?"

"What do you mean?"

"In your statement you said you'd seen Ken and Florence at my house "at least ten times". He didn't come round here more than three or four times in all, and you certainly weren't present every time. So how is that even possible?"

This slowed him down a little, but I could still hear him breathing hard at the other end of the line. It was an unpleasant moment.

"Alright, I admit that may have been a mistake."

"Damn right it was. Now they think we must have lived in each other's pockets for years. Imagine how that looks, especially after what I told them. If you want me to tell the police I got it wrong about you, then you're going to have to tell them you got it wrong about how often you saw Ken and Florence at my house. Right?" There was a pause. Now we were both breathing heavily. Finally the tension eased, and we agreed to contact our respective solicitors and put the record straight. As it happened, Mark Crowley attached little significance to our mistakes. His view was that, in view of the lengthy passage of time, more than twenty-five years, the jury would be unlikely to hold either of our accounts to strict scrutiny, and it would weaken the Prosecution's case if they attempted to hector us about it. Once I learned this the relief was overwhelming. Our friendship had survived a real test, and a subsequent phone call found us on as amicable terms as ever. Nothing more was said about our 'false statements', but as had been the case with Liz and me, an unspoken deal was struck in which we would be gentle with each other from now on, whatever happened.

Chapter Thirteen

*Life is like a shit sandwich: the thicker the bread,
the less shit you taste – Anon*

Monday the seventeenth of July, 2017, ten am. The cleaners have come and gone; I have just come back from a delightful walk in the morning sun to carry out a couple of errands. I popped to the bakers to buy a large granary loaf and a square of chocolate shortbread. Having made myself a coffee (the second of six today), I am ready to start writing.

For reasons I cannot explain I feel good this morning. Britain has awoken to the news that there is to be a female Dr Who. There is also talk of replacing Daniel Craig's 007 with a younger model. Idris Elba appears to be the people's choice, but may I suggest Riz Ahmed? He is ten years younger than Elba and *so* hot right now, especially in America. Come to that, you could push the envelope even further and have a female Bond: Vicky McClure perhaps?

The weather is set fair, low humidity, temperature in the mid twenties: in other words the very definition of a perfect summer's day in Wales.

But there are one or two flies in my lip salve. First, where are the flying ants? This should be their day. Maybe I am worrying unnecessarily; the day is yet young. Perhaps they will make their appearance later. And of course they don't always swarm on this day. Sometimes they miss a whole year when the conditions are not to their liking. But I won't feel completely relaxed until I see my first one take to the air. Come to that, where are their nemesis, the swifts? I can remember a time, and not so long ago, when throughout the summer they would swarm above our house in their hundreds. This year there is barely a handful of them to be seen.

Second, my eczema usually recedes in the summer months,[26] but this year it has failed to do so. Hardly surprising, I suppose. Also, the annoying little bubble in my left eye is still extant, and has been now for a full week. Next week I go the eye clinic for my regular check, and I wait with some anxiety to hear the specialist's views on it. My wife wants to come with me, "Just for moral support", though I suspect it is because she doesn't want me to be alone should the worst happen, and they inform me this is the first sign my corneal transplant is beginning to break down.

As for my other little problem, I have been in a moderately bullish mood about it for several days. This has enabled me to enjoy Wimbledon almost like in the old days, unlike last year when it passed me by in a blur of undiluted fear. Of course that does not mean I do not wake several times each night and worry, and it remains the first thing on my mind when I awake each morning.

Perhaps it has something to do with the fact that a team of lawyers is assembling to take on my defence, and they seem pretty good. On the advice of my solicitor, Mark Crowley, I have employed the services of a female barrister called Susan Ferrier. She is known in the trade as a 'junior', though the term is a misnomer. 'Junior' simply means that a barrister is not a QC. Sue Ferrier was called to the bar twenty-five years ago and has a formidable record defending people charged with historical sexual assault. She makes an excellent first impression: quietly spoken, unassuming almost, good looking in a typical Welsh manner, clean, even features, large, kindly brown eyes and long dark hair. I wonder how she will look on the day she confronts my accuser in court.

At our first meeting it was immediately apparent she had done her homework on my case thoroughly. She had read through all one thousand five hundred pages of witness statements, and had some interesting observations:

"First, there is the sheer number of interviews with the complainant, sixteen if memory serves. In my experience that is almost unprecedented. In almost every case of this kind I have ever seen, there is only one interview. It may stretch over several

---

26 Only to recur with renewed vigour once the central heating comes on again.

days, as this complainant's have, but usually it all comes out in one go. In this case, there is a steady ramping up as the interviews proceed, with more offenders implicated and the seriousness of the accusations escalating."

A lengthy discussion follows which attempts to make some sort of sense out of all this.

"Which brings me to my next point. What of Florence's mother? There is no statement from her in the pack the CPS provided. Did she even make one? Clearly she is in an invidious position. If she, who is clearly a highly intelligent and sophisticated woman, who holds down a responsible job, failed to recognise the signs of abuse in her own daughter and continued to send her to her father, what kind of mother does that make her? Alternatively, if she does *not* believe Florence was abused, she risks alienating her daughter if she says so. In either of these scenarios she is unlikely to emerge well, so it may be that she declined to give a statement to the police. But we will find out soon enough."

'Unused material' refers to information held by the CPS which they have decided is not of value to the prosecution, and therefore, by implication, may be of assistance to the defence: interviews with witnesses which confirm my account of the events, photographs which may be of exculpatory value, and other things which may come as a complete surprise. The judge sets a timetable for when this material should be released to the defence, though, as Sue Ferrier warns me, the CPS are often dilatory in handing them over. But sooner or later they will have to divulge all they have. Then she moves on to the next issue.

"In view of the seriousness of the charges you face, there may be an argument for asking for the services of a leading counsel. Of course this will not be cheap, but you must be aware you face a series of very serious charges. Plus, you know how it is, two heads are better than one."

Not cheap is right. When Ched Evans retained eminent London silk Judy Khan to run his successful appeal against his rape conviction, his legal expenses ran to several hundred thousand pounds. But he is a wealthy professional footballer; I am not. That is a great deal more money than I have at *my* disposal. Fortunately the QC she has in mind will charge only a fraction of that, though it is quite a *large* fraction. She suggests I go home and discuss the issue with my wife, but it doesn't take us long to decide. What is it worth to secure one's freedom? The answer, of course, is whatever is necessary. And while it is infuriating to think that only a small percentage of it will be refunded even if I am found not guilty, we don't want to find ourselves later regretting we conducted our defence on the cheap and got what we paid for. On the other hand, it may not be necessary to drain my funds completely. To put it this way, you might wish to spend every penny you had buying a Bentley or an Aston Martin, but a high end Audi or BMW would probably serve your purposes just as well.

There is also the question of finding someone with whom Sue Ferrier feels happy to collaborate. Another QC is suggested, a man with a formidable reputation; a man capable of striking fear into the hearts of prosecuting counsel and even judges. But he is also known for his 'abrasive personality', and therefore someone Sue Ferrier might not feel comfortable to work alongside. Moreover, a QC from her own chambers would reduce costs, whereas the 'Rottweiler' they referred to works elsewhere. Again, money always matters.

Finally, I am asked whose name appears on the deeds of my house. Since I bought it in 1984, I tell them, the house has been solely in my name.

"You might want to think about changing that. In the unlikely event[27] of your being found guilty, and, in fact, even if you are acquitted, Florence could sue you through the civil courts and possibly win substantial damages. Unless you add your wife's name to the deed of ownership, or even transfer full ownership to her, you risk losing your house."

There and then I instruct my solicitor to draw up papers transferring full ownership of the house to Liz. In the 'unlikely event' of us divorcing, I would still be entitled to half of the equity, and there is no way I am going to let Florence take my house from me as well as my freedom.

As I write these words today I begin to realise why I am feeling better than I have for a long time. For so long my outlook has been dominated by fear, but it seems to me now that this is

---

27 A nice phrase. Sue Ferrier has so far been reluctant to say *how* unlikely.

slowly being replaced by anger, a growing rage at the injustice to which I have been subjected. I have never in any way hurt the woman who accuses me now of so many terrible crimes, yet I have already been severely punished: arrested at Bristol airport and placed in handcuffs; held for a night in solitary confinement, and then subjected to a prolonged period of stress and anxiety, during which I have fallen prey to all manner of stress-related ailments. I have not allowed it to destroy me, but it has placed a dark shadow over my life for more than a year. Too damn right I'm angry. Anger is not usually thought of as a positive emotion, but there is one beautiful thing about it: it banishes fear. It isn't so long ago I thought fear was overwhelming my ability to express or even feel anger. Not any more.

But later it turns out the feeling is transitory; as often as not I remain in a state of persistent, gnawing anxiety.

*

A few days later I left a message for my solicitor: go ahead and employ the services of a QC, whoever they decide is best suited to being my 'leading counsel'. What will follow is characterised by him as a 'beauty parade': putting the case out for tender, with Mark Crowley and Sue Ferrier acting as judges. I'm happy to leave the decision to them. They know a lot more about it than I do.

In the weeks following the first meeting with my barrister I decided to become better acquainted with the numerous interviews Florence had given to the police over the course of several years. I have to admit that initially I had pretty much skip-read them, so shocking were the contents. To hear someone accusing you of committing the most disgusting crimes over and over again was almost too much to bear. Upon re-reading the interviews, however, certain interesting facts revealed themselves that I had overlooked on the first read-through. But they were no less upsetting for that.

Chapter Fourteen

Assaults in prisons in England and Wales in the year ending March 2017: 26,643 incidents, including 6 murders – 20% up on the previous year – *Office for National Statistics*

"Knock knock! Ah, good. The doctor is in I see."

"What's happening guys?"

"Oh, we're just doing a little house call type of thing. OK Jeffrey, put him on his bed and hold him still."

"I don't like to be called Jeffrey. I prefer Jeff."

"Ooh, picky!"

"Get off me! What are you doing?"

"Shut up. OK, let's get those keks off. Ooh, Calvin Klein pants! Classy! I guess you won't be needing those for a while. God, what a tiny little prick he's got. It's always the same with these pervs. Well, it's gonna be a lot smaller in a minute. You got the turps Jimmy? OK, pour it on. Don't be stingy with it, use the whole fucking bottle. And don't splash it about you berk! Some of that went on me!"

"Look guys. You're making a terrible mistake. I didn't do anything to that girl. It was all lies."

"Ah, right, you're only here coz you got screwed by your lawyer, right?"

"Please guys, don't do this. *Please.*"

"Will you listen to him? I bet that girl begged him to stop, just like that. Look, *doctor*, the jury found you guilty, right? So they didn't believe you. And here's the news, pal, Neither do we. Kiddy-fiddling, rape, even did an abortion on her I heard. Well, your dick's going to look like an abortion in a minute. Pass us the matches. And hold him still will you?"

"No! For God's sake no!"

"Now, doctor. Here's a little taste of what we do to sick little perverts like you. And remember this: if we ever see you on this floor again we'll cut your hands off so you'll never be able to touch a little girl again. And after that we'll poke your eyes out so you won't be able to look at one either. Here we go. Oh my God will you look at that? It's beautiful! OK, you coming Jeffrey?"

"I told you, it's Jeff. And I wanna watch him burn a bit longer."

I wake up screaming. Bathed in sweat and fear, I have thrown off all my bedclothes, and my body appears to be radiating heat. Liz, terrified herself, attempts to comfort me. Once again I pretend to remember nothing of my nightmare.

Wednesday the nineteenth of July 2017, ten am. My unexpected good mood has evaporated. The fear is back again. It seems I got the timetable slightly wrong. I thought the next 'bundle' to be released by the CPS was going to be the Unused Material, evidence they have gathered which they do not feel strengthens their case, and therefore may strengthen ours. It now appears that the next pack will contain additional evidence which they have not released thus far, which they think *does* strengthen their case. What will it contain? There won't be any evidence of me having interfered with any young girls or children, because I have never done anything of the kind. But after what has already emerged I am prepared for almost anything.

Have they been to the Health Authority, and obtained a list of complaints made against me over the years? They'll find nothing to do with sexual impropriety, but plenty of complaints about my somewhat unconventional approach. None of them ever came to anything; I was never fined or censured in any way, but they will find several letters complaining about my attitude. One patient, for example, accused me of being "The rudest man in Cardiff", after I had refused her demands to give her a prescription of temazepam before it was due. Perhaps they will use it as further evidence of my 'bad character'.

Then there is the issue of my late son's medical notes. Last autumn I tried to access them, just in case they might contain something of exculpatory value. After a lengthy delay I was eventually told by the medical records office that they were missing, or at least most of them were. Crucially, all the hospital notes from 2006, when he spent several months in a locked psychiatric unit after a schizophrenic breakdown, had vanished. They admitted that *someone* had requested the notes, but had not returned them. They refused to divulge who had removed them, when it had happened or why. The most likely candidates would be the doctors involved in his care at the time, probably for research purposes. But perhaps the police took out a court order, and have been sifting through them, line by line, to see if my boy said anything incriminating about me. How reliable such evidence would be, in light of the fact that he had completely lost touch with reality by then, is hard to say.

Then there is my computer. There is the 'Sirens of the Silver Screen' collection gathered over the years, and about which I may be worrying over nothing. But there are also numerous documents, examples of creative writing I produced before this ever happened. My autobiography makes frequent mention of my drug use in a far-off era.

It is a long tradition in medicine for doctors experimenting on themselves to explore the effects of drugs and previously untested medicines, and I can argue that it was in that spirit of 'research' that I took these drugs. And I'll admit it: I had a lot of fun too. My use was limited; it was carefully controlled, but there can be little doubt that the prosecution will use this, if they find it, to suggest I am some sort of out-of-control druggie; a serial law-breaker, someone capable of committing almost any crime. Including the ones of which I am now accused.

All I know for sure is that they will use anything they can to blacken my character. Maybe it will be material no one on my defence team has even anticipated; something they call the "nasty little surprise". Maybe it will be devastating to my defence. I just don't know. Which is why I'm afraid again.

I hope to feel a little better soon. At the end of the month my wife Liz and I are off to spend four days on the Isle of Man. It was one of the holiday locations we planned in the event of my passport being seized. As it turned out it wasn't, but we decided to go anyway. It has several megalithic remains, a couple of medieval castles, miles of sandy beaches, mountains; even a museum of steam! Our cup runneth over. All we need is for the weather to be set fair, and even that doesn't trouble my wife:

"I don't care what the weather does! I'm going to enjoy it, whatever."

The only thing she *is* a bit worried about is the ferry crossing. It takes nearly three hours, and she isn't a great sailor. Better stock up on sea-sickness pills, and do my best to put my problems behind me, at least for a few days…

★

Monday the twenty-fourth of July 2017, three pm. I am just returned from the eye clinic, where I saw my ophthalmologist, Mr Vinod Kumar. I am fortunate to have such a man looking after my eyes. By sheer coincidence he happens to be one of the world's leading authorities on Fuchs' syndrome, and it was he who performed my left corneal transplant back in January 2014. I think the word which best describes him is 'dapper'. About five feet eight inches in height and possessing not an ounce of body fat, he is always attired in a perfectly fitting pinstripe suit, and his hands are beautifully manicured. His dark eyes radiate a kindly twinkle, but behind them lies a fierce intelligence. And his dexterity is legendary. After he had performed my transplant, one of his juniors was examining the result a few weeks later and marvelled at the quality of his handiwork:

"It's remarkable", she said. "Fourteen tiny, perfect stitches, and all of them in less than an inch!"

Today he identified the cause of my strange oval-shaped floater immediately: apparently it is a 'Weiss Ring'[28] and is diagnostic of a partial posterior vitreous detachment, no less. Accompanied by a series of bright flashes, known in the trade as 'photopsia', on the periphery of the vision as the vitreous humour pulls away from the retina, a small 'bubble' is left in the vision, marking the position of the optic nerve root. Did I notice any coloured flashes on the periphery of my vision just before the bubble appeared? Yes, as it happens, I did. They were very odd. To experience something like this under the influence of an

---

28 Pronounced 'vice', it now seems even my diseases are ironic.

hallucinogenic, say, magic mushrooms, is understandable; to come out of the blue was more than a little scary.

He examined the back of my eye (annoyingly, it had happened in my 'good' eye, the one in which I had had the corneal transplant), and announced:

"Nothing to worry about then, just a sign of ageing", he said breezily; then, on my asking how long my infuriating little bubble may be expected to persist, he replied:

"Oh, they're usually permanent."

Without giving me time to react, he then added:

"Look out for more photopsia though, and get up here straight away if they occur. They may indicate imminent retinal detachment. The first six weeks is when you are most at risk."

He calls that "nothing to worry about"? Retinal detachment *is* dangerous. Today it can often be repaired, but sometimes it may result in blindness in the affected eye. Remember that thing about God only giving you what He knows you can cope with? Bollocks. He is not content with giving me a mother gradually imploding under the effects of dementia, and a woman intent on seeing me spend the rest of my life behind bars. Now He gives me the distinct possibility of going blind in my one good eye. And a little fly that is going to follow my vision wherever it goes. Forever. If I believed in God I wouldn't be too pleased with him right now. Perhaps it is just as well I don't.

All I know for certain at this moment is that my life is pressing in on me with an unbearable weight.

*

This morning, partly to distract myself from dwelling on what I might be told at the eye clinic later in the day, I started re-reading the 'Notes for PTPH' (Pre-Trial Preparation Hearing) issued by the CPS just before my appearance at Crown Court on the sixteenth of June 2017. In essence it was a summary of the case against the accused. It offers an intriguing thumbnail sketch of myself during the early 1990s:

'*He was a close friend of Ken D* (Florence's father). *He knew*

Owen H.[29] *He was associated for some time with a circus before ultimately working as a General Practitioner.*[30] *He had a reputation within the alternative scene as being a go-to man for unconventional therapies and remedies.'*

Fascinating stuff. It is as if my interest in circus skills and alternative medicine are somehow suspicious – signs perhaps of some sort of degenerate, morally dubious character, untrustworthy and perhaps capable of child abuse, torture, rape and illegal abortion. But the truth is there is *nothing* wrong with having juggling as one of my hobbies, and I am *proud* of my use of alternative medicine to reduce the amount of drugs I prescribed as a GP. In 1993 we won "Cardiff Practice of the Year", due in no small part to our very low prescribing levels. Over the years we saved the NHS a small fortune. And alternative medicine was a part of that.

One of the prosecution witnesses knew me, and it was from her police statement they found the description of me as a 'go-to' guy for alternative medicine. She said she had visited Diana, Florence's mother, on one occasion, and found her giving her daughter steam inhalation treatment for a heavy cold. When she learned it was me who had suggested the idea, it impressed her because I, a doctor, had recommended a form of treatment which did not involve using drugs. She confirmed that she had attended one or two of those parties herself, and agreed with my description of them as platforms for lively political debates which often went on long into the night. In other words nothing like the depraved orgies the police had decided they were. Despite all this she is named as a prosecution witness. From what she has said, I should have thought she could be used a *defence* witness.

As for Ken himself, the alleged architect of all the abuse, she described him as a likeable man "if not wholly respectable", whom she was happy to use as a babysitter for her young son on several occasions. This child liked Ken and was perfectly happy

29 They have this the wrong way round. I *knew* Ken, though as I said in my police interview, he was not in the 'inner circle' of my friends. Owen, on the other hand, *was* one of my closest friends.

30 Wrong again. I had been working as a GP for eight years *before* I met the circus people who taught me to juggle.

to go with him. Toddlers may not always be able to communicate in conventional ways, but they *are* able to convey their likes and dislikes, and what they are afraid of, in ways which leaves no one in any doubt as to how they feel.

Chapter Fifteen

The Isle of Man is the omphalos of the British Isles
– *John Michell*

Wednesday the second of August 2017, five pm. I am in Douglas, on the Isle of Man, sitting in my hotel room on the third floor (sixty-six steps up from street level, no lift). Our hotel is situated on the promenade, facing east towards the Cumbrian coast. On an exceptionally clear day, it is said, one can see Scafell Pike, fifty miles distant, standing tall amongst the peaks of the Lake District. Below me, a horse-drawn tram clip-clops past. I feel sorry for the horse, for there is only one to pull the tram, which may carry as many as twenty passengers. But it seems to manage with equanimity; once the inertia is overcome it maintains a steady walking pace, and at least there are no inclines to negotiate.

My wife and I are resting after the adventures of the day before venturing out to the nearby chippy.

Yesterday was a delightful summer's day, and we took advantage of the clement weather to climb Snaefell, the island's high point. From its summit, though only when viewing conditions are perfect, it is possible to see all four nations of the United Kingdom. On this occasion a fine haze prevented us from seeing across the Irish Sea to the far-off coasts, though the whole island was laid out before us; its craggy coastline and patchwork of meadows and sunny uplands, and a procession of dark mountains threading their way along its spine.

It was an unpleasant pull up the steep slopes of Snaefell, though I think it was only while puffing and panting my way up there that I forgot about my problems altogether. Once I had recovered from the two hundred and twenty metre ascent, we made the far easier descent[31] and then journeyed on to the ancient town of Peel on the east coast, following the route of the famous TT course. Wandering the stately ruins of its castle, bathed in dazzling sunshine, I contemplated the history of this unique place. Home to a pre-Celtic civilisation since the end of the last Ice Age, they left their mark with a variety of unique megalithic tombs and chambered cairns. Late in the first millennium it became the southernmost outpost of the Viking 'Kingdom of the Isles', and King Magnus built the first fortifications at Peel in the early eleventh century.

The island was wrested from the Vikings by Scottish king Alexander III a hundred years later, but they in turn had to give it up to the English in 1331. In 1406 Henry IV gifted it to the Stanley family, hereditary Earls of Derby, who controlled it as absent, if relatively benevolent landlords for over three hundred years.

Centuries of running their own affairs has left the Manx people fiercely protective of their independence from the mainland, and this is now enshrined in law: they set their own taxes, far lower than in the rest of the UK, and while there are speed limits on the roads, there are no speed cameras anywhere on the island. "They tried putting a couple up", a resident told me, "but the locals burned them down in the night. After that they stopped bothering."

By the following morning the weather had turned. Sunny skies were replaced by mist and low cloud, sometimes a gentle, hesitant drizzle; sometimes by what the weather forecasters like to call 'pulses' of steady, driving rain. Undaunted, we made our way to the south-western corner of the island to find the Mull Hill stone circle, near the tiny village of Craigneash. Ancient monuments are not well signposted here, but our ordnance survey map pointed the way until high on a deserted, mist-wrapped road we thought we must be close. I noticed a solitary car, a battered old Morris Minor, parked in a lay-by and approached the occupant. A little reluctantly he wound down his window at my discreet knock.

---

31 Most people report steep descents being harder than ascents, but then they probably don't have COPD.

"Excuse me. Do you know if there is a stone circle near here?"

"Aye, it's up the hill by that path there," he replied, pointing to one of three paths disappearing up the hill into the gloom.

"It's a seven minute walk but you'll get yourselves drenched."

His accent was odd; it had a hint of Irish in it, a touch of Liverpool too, but something else that rendered it unique to my ears. Perhaps his was the famous 'Manx' dialect, often spoken of but rarely encountered by tourists. We went to where the paths began, but I wasn't sure which one he had pointed to. Seeing our indecision he jumped out of his car and scuttled over to us. He was tiny, barely five feet tall, and with his straggly white beard bore more than a passing resemblance to Old Father Time, minus the scythe. He pointed to the correct path and repeated himself:

"Seven minutes up the hill, but you'll be drenched."

We thanked him and set off. The path soon degenerated into a barely visible track through a gorse thicket; its spines raked at our legs mercilessly as we stumbled through it. But he was right: seven minutes later we got to the top of the hill and found the circle, which we soon found was not a circle at all, but a series of six chambered tombs now open to the elements, arranged in a circular pattern. It was nothing like any ancient site I have seen before. The array of white stones, blotched here and there with patches of yellow lichen, seemed almost luminous in the pale light as the sun struggled to break through the mist. The little man was right about the drenching though. Striding through the dense undergrowth left our trousers soaked through, and the clinging drizzle completed the job.

By the time we got back to the car he had vanished. Who was he? One of the Manx Little People? Certainly the tradition for them is as strong here as it is in neighbouring Ireland. I felt sad he'd gone. I had wanted to thank him for helping us find the site, which without his assistance would have been difficult if not impossible.

The holiday ended on an unfortunate note. Somewhere on the journey home I lost my camera, along with the two hundred-odd pictures on its SD card. *Where were you when you last had it?* is the usual refrain in such situations, and that is easy to answer: I was on the observation deck of the car ferry, photographing a forest of offshore wind turbines in Liverpool Bay. I contacted the lost property department of the shipping line the following day, but nothing had been handed in. I tried the motorway services where we had stopped on the drive home to buy sandwiches: nothing there either. It has gone.

The Buddhists teach us that all things are impermanent: we should not become overly attached to material objects, which are often replaceable in any case. But photographs are *not* replaceable. They are lost forever, and some of them were very good: the ancient sites, the castles, the hillsides embroidered with marvellous patterns of purple and yellow from the heather and gorse, mist lying low over receding mountain ridges. We would have to go again to replace these, and even then it would not be the same. The past cannot be recaptured.

Losing something precious is a bit like grief; the denial, the despair, the anger, the yearning for that which cannot be retrieved. And finally, the acceptance.

Which took a while.

Freud reminds us that there are no accidents: there are always reasons why things happen. I have a theory to explain why I lost my camera: I was having too good a time. Ever since my son died I have felt uncomfortable about enjoying myself too much. It is as if I do not have the right to be truly happy in a world where he no longer exists, and if it begins to look like I am, I do something about it. Even today I am haunted by the suspicion that had I been a better parent, had I *loved* him more, he might still be alive today. No one who knows and cares for me accepts this theory. But what do they know?

A postscript to our holiday on the Isle of Man. One reason we were able to have such a (relatively) carefree time was that just before our departure, my solicitor sent us the CPS's second bundle of disclosures, and thank God, there is little if anything new in it to threaten my freedom. The previously handwritten statements from witnesses are now typed, as per the judge's instructions, and Florence's interviews have been heavily redacted to remove most of the references to her father. Again, this was on the instructions of the judge, who pointed out that as he is not on trial, having disappeared nearly twenty years ago, there seems little point in burdening the jury with pages and pages of accounts of his depravity towards her. Of course some of it will have to remain: according to her, Ken was the instigator, the prime mover of all the abuse, inviting, according to her, anything up to ten men (several of whom are now dead) to violate her, one by one or in a group. We are not accused of acting together, remember; he was the sole link between us all. So he will have to be mentioned at some point, though a lot more briefly than might otherwise have been the case. Whether this will help the accused is uncertain, but it will make the jury's job slightly easier. Interestingly, there is still no statement from Florence's mother, nor are there any transcripts of interviews with my late son's friends.

Chapter Sixteen

They say a little learning is a dangerous thing: imagine how much
trouble a lot can cause. – *Tom Sharpe, Porterhouse Blue*

August the twenty-seventh 2017, ten am. It is eleven years to the
day since we found my son's lifeless body in his flat. And to mark
that day, every year since we have journeyed to the western
region of the Brecon Beacons, to immerse ourselves in a beautiful little plunge pool, fed by a tiny, tinkling waterfall.

Sheltering under the dark bulk of Fan Brycheiniog, which
towers eight hundred metres above the sea, lies the little lake of
Llyn y Fan Fawr, and from this lake a stream tumbles down the
mountain in a series of rock pools and waterfalls. A mile
downstream it joins the headwaters of the River Tawe, which
finds its way to the sea thirty miles away at Swansea, whose
Welsh name is *Abertawe*, "the mouth of the Tawe".[32]

This is a magical place. On the other side of the mountain
ridge lies Llyn y Fan Fawr's sister lake, Llyn y Fan Fach, associated since antiquity with the legend of the Lady of the Lake,
while all around us, standing stones dot the landscape.

We brought our son here long ago, and mortified him by
removing our clothes and plunging into its cool, but infinitely
refreshing waters. As the years passed he got used to our strange
ways, and eventually even joined us and jumped in himself. Now
we come here every year to plunge, and to make small offerings
to his spirit. This year we have chosen three of his favourite
treats: half a pound of Double Gloucester cheese, a fistful of
jelly-beans and a Walnut Whip.

---

32 The River Tawe was gifted to the Duke of Beaufort by Charles II in the late 17th
century. The current duke still owns it, and everything in it. It has been a highly
lucrative acquisition: in 2008 he levied £280,000 from Swansea City Council for
their use of the river.

It is a perfect late summer morning, just as it was the day we discovered his body all those years ago. Often it is cool up here at over five hundred metres above sea level, but today conditions are divine, nearly twenty degrees, with a gentle, warming breeze. And the water, normally so bracing, is today almost warm. As we are drying ourselves off and putting our clothes back on, Liz notices something in the water. There, glittering in the deepest part of the pool, is a woman's gold necklace. Could someone else be using this place for ritualistic purposes?

On the way back down to the car we notice a slowworm basking on a rock, making the most of the unaccustomed warmth. It slithers quickly away into cover when it senses our approach. Its skin is a lustrous, golden colour, indicating it is not yet fully mature. Left undisturbed in the wild slowworms can live to over forty years. My son alas did not achieve even half that: he was just nineteen when he died.

Our little outing has taken our minds off our current preoccupation, sifting through the second, and much larger bundle of Unused Materials, supplied last week by the CPS. Now at last we can read the interviews with Seth's friends, none of whom reported him ever saying anything about my having abused him. As a matter of fact some of them were kind enough to contact me and report the gist of their police interviews, and they were all pretty angry they had been troubled in this way about their late buddy, unanimous in rejecting any suggestion of abuse on my part.

As we trawl through the files, I wonder: will we find evidence of previous false allegations of sexual assault made by Florence? If she has made even one, the prosecution's case against me would be seriously weakened. And if she made more than one...

Then there are the notes made by Florence's psychotherapist. These notes, covering the two hundred and twenty-nine sessions Florence had with her over a three-and-a-half year period between 2007 and 2011, have taken me nearly three days to read in their entirety. What emerges most strongly is a pattern of escalating claims of abuse as the sessions mount up. Florence must have represented a formidable challenge to her therapist, a challenge which her therapist clearly found increasingly difficult to manage.

There are also some references to 'regression therapy', though I am willing to admit I skip-read them. I don't know much about the technique, except that it has been associated with the creation of 'false memories'. It is all so upsetting I am probably not doing a very good job of reviewing. Good thing more impartial eyes will be poring over it for me.

What is not included are innumerable emails, phone calls and text messages that also passed between them, though the defence will be demanding they too be handed over, if, that is, they are still available. What we have already, however, is deeply shocking.

Amongst others, there is the story where she claimed I forced her to digitally penetrate my own son, while I sat watching with an "evil smile" on my face. Such a tale sounds as if it could have come straight out of Ian Brady's playbook, and on hearing it one can easily imagine a jury member running from the court and vomiting in a corridor. It is hard to believe any jury could accept that such a thing really happened; nonetheless, these allegations *do* form part of the charges I face, so it will be put to them. The CPS has distilled the "child torture" incidents into six separate charges, under the umbrella term of "Inducing a child to commit an act of gross indecency". But however hard it is to believe any jury is going to buy any of these appalling allegations, I have to bear in mind what Sue Ferrier said, namely that you can never predict how a jury's collective mind is going to work.

I have also taken on the task of scrutinising her GP notes. They are so voluminous it takes me nearly three days. Obviously I am forbidden by the rules of Contempt of Court, to say nothing of preserving the confidentiality of the patient, to reveal any details of what I found. But I think I can say that they do give the lie to one of Florence's statements, namely that my abuse of her "destroyed her faith in the medical profession". Maybe so, but it clearly didn't stop her consulting members of that profession on many, many occasions. Which is not to say that regular attenders *trust* their doctors. In my experience, all too often the reverse is the case. "I went to the doctors hundreds of times" they will say, "But they never really helped me, never really understood me." Not infrequently they end up *hating* doctors.

The medical notes are by no means complete. There are

several years of files missing, and no midwife's notes at all. Perhaps they will be supplied later.[33]

The files also contain details of the police tactics and strategy in pursuing *Operation Violet Oak*. Unknown to us, the police had been actively pursuing their investigation, albeit with some substantial gaps, since early in 2013. The first we knew anything was amiss was the thirtieth of June 2016, the 'Day of Action' as they called it, when they swooped on four of the accused, one of them at his workplace, one about to attend a hospital appointment (he was permitted to attend his appointment in the event, accompanied by two burly police officers), and took them away for interrogation. It should have been five, but I spoiled their party by being in Vienna on the day in question. I never told them where I was; only that I was out of the country. However, using investigative techniques which you have to admit are pretty impressive, they worked out exactly when and where I was due to return to the UK, and, as we have seen, lifted me at Bristol airport. It now emerges I was the only one they hand-cuffed, and the only one they kept in the cells overnight.

Finally there are records of contacts between Florence and the investigating police officers. A lot is missing; many text messages and emails are still not yet released, but what has been made available shows, to say the least, an unusual relationship between them. It seems they are acting more as therapists than police officers carrying out an objective investigation. 'Hi hon!' is how several emails from the lead officer begin. There are hardly any challenges to what Florence is saying; it is simply recorded with scarcely any follow-up questions. Psychotherapists are trained to believe everything their clients tell them, however outlandish it might be. The police, you would have thought, are not permitted that luxury, but it has been clear from the outset that the police have believed *everything* they have been told.

Going through all these files is draining both emotionally and physically, but it must be done. Only in this material will we find the inconsistencies in her account we can use to challenge her version of events.

---

33 They never were.

*

Wednesday the thirtieth of August 2017, five pm. Five months to go. The dream team assembles. I am at my lawyer's offices, waiting to meet my 'leading counsel', my 'Silk', for the first time.

Mark Crowley is tall, lean, and obviously very fit. His face has the curious ability to convey sternness and kindliness at the same time. As I enter his office, he is sitting in the 'captain's chair' behind his huge desk, scowling at a huge sheaf of papers, but when he sees me he jumps up to shake my hand. My barrister, Susan Ferrier is not here yet, while Christopher Clee, QC, has phoned ahead to say he is stuck in traffic on the M4 and may be up to an hour late. In an attempt to ease the tension, Mark relates a story from twenty years ago, when he was called by the police in the small hours to see a Mark Crowley they had arrested.

"There must be some mistake, officer. This is Mark Crowley speaking."

"I know sir, and we have one Mark Crowley in our cells now, and he wishes to see the duty solicitor."

I respond that although my own name is unusual, years ago at my son's suggestion, I had googled my name and found there were actually eight Stephen (or Steven) Glascoes in Britain. There was, however, only one Seth Glascoe: him. And now, I imagine, none at all.

After a few minutes Sue Ferrier is ushered into the office, and Mark gives up his captain's seat to her and sits on my side of the desk. I notice her large brown eyes twinkle as she greets me. Finally Mr Clee arrives, and Sue in turn hands over her chair to him and joins us on the other side of the desk. He is immensely tall, with a good head of slightly tousled, greying hair, and penetrating grey-blue eyes. The general effect is matter-of-fact, even down to earth. A little to my surprise, his voice does not have the clipped, patrician tones one might have expected of a QC; he speaks in an easy, straightforward way with perhaps a trace of a northern accent. I can see why Sue Ferrier said he tends to go down well with juries. When he catches your eye, however, his look is disturbing. It is hard to dissemble in his presence. Some of his questions are surprising. What was my life like after my wife died in 1990? How, for instance, did I manage to juggle my child care with my life as a full-time GP? I have to think for a moment. Then the detail comes back. I used a nursery situated just down the street during surgery hours, and a small but loyal cadre of family and friends to baby-sit him at other times. By 1992 he was attending infants school, which made the situation slightly easier. As regards my private life, I had several girlfriends, as part of a larger plan to find a suitable 'replacement Mum' for my son. He seems to be satisfied with my response.

There follows a technical discussion between the lawyers which is well beyond my sphere of comprehension. It is as if I am not there at all, even though it is me and my fate that is being thrashed out in front of me. There is talk of 'section 78', and 'section 41'. There is a strange moment when my mind flips back fifty years and I am in a hospital bed, aged twelve, with a cluster of doctors standing around my bed discussing my case. I have the temerity to ask them what they are talking about.

"Be quiet, young man. This is *nothing* to do with *you*."

I let the lawyers converse without interruption. At last there is a brief lull which gives me time to tell them of my principal concern: how will the prosecution go about attacking me on the stand? Chris Clee fixes me with his gaze and asks:

"Were you *addicted* to cannabis, LSD or any other drugs at any time?"

I look directly into his eyes and reply:

"No."

He nods, satisfied, and then, a little to my surprise says no more about it and moves on to talk about the inconsistencies in Florence's story. There is no shortage of them, he says. How could there not be, with all those thousands of words spun out over so many separate interviews? It is easy to be consistent when one is relating the plain truth. Far more difficult when one is weaving a complex web of narratives. And while on cross examination she could, like the defendants, claim that her memory for distant events is understandably patchy, or that inconsistencies could simply be down to exhaustion (it is true some of her interviews lasted hours), there are uncomfortable facts about her past she will not be able to refute so easily.

He explains how the various barristers for the defence (there are five of them in all) intend to collaborate so that they do not end up asking the same questions over and over. When the time for the trial approaches they will get together to decide which one will go after her on each and every weak spot in her story, hoping to avoid the charge that they are badgering her. This is a real risk, because they cannot afford to let the jury start feeling sorry for her by getting the feeling she is being bullied.

Chris Clee continues with his agenda. The important task for the defence, he says, is to create a comprehensive timeline of events and statements, one that pulls in *all* the interviews Florence gave, *all* the statements from "witnesses",[34] *all* the medical notes and counselling records, and merges them into a single, coherent whole. Only by creating this will we be able to mount an effective counter to her allegations. Thankfully, that will be their job. I have already submitted my observations on the unused materials; the *merging* job is theirs. They may get an independent expert in to review the whole thing to cast an opinion as to her mental state and reliability, as well as another medical expert to refute her account of the abortion she claims I performed on her.

"Is that OK with you?" he asks. He doesn't spell it out, but it is clear these 'experts' will cost a lot of money. *My* money.

"I'm willing to do whatever it takes to get a not guilty verdict on all charges," I reply.

"Good answer", he says with a grin. And then the meeting is over. Throughout the exchanges I have been itching to ask him the question which has been on my mind since the beginning of this nightmare: "What do you think my chances are?"

I manage to prevent myself. Maybe I am afraid of his answer, which might have been anything from: "Oh, I think we have an excellent chance of acquittal" to "If I'm honest, it could go either way. It's impossible to predict with any confidence."

Perhaps just as well I kept my mouth shut.

Despite the lingering sense of uncertainty, I walk home

---

34 Of course there were no *eyewitnesses*. The term refers to the various people, boyfriends, woman friends, counsellors, doctors and others, to whom she spoke about her alleged abuse

feeling better about the whole situation than I have for months. And perhaps that is what I am paying for.

★

Friday the eighth of September 2017, eleven am. The MA course is officially over. The last formal teaching I had was a lengthy session with my academic supervisor, Richard Gwyn, way back on the thirtieth of June. But throughout the summer I have been tinkering with my stories and essays, changing a word here, altering a sentence construction there, until I reached that point, familiar to every writer, where I started second-guessing myself, and finding that an alteration I made was not as good as what I had down already. That's when you have to stop and admit to yourself: "In the time allowed, this is as good as I can make it".

Today I submitted my second and final portfolio; this time of ten thousand words, comprising two fictional short stories and four nonfiction pieces. Once again it will be over a month before I find out my mark, and also to learn if I have passed the course and am able to put the letters "MA" after my name. Not that I am worried about failing. Whereas at medical school, where the bottom ten per cent were failed each year, I was told right at the beginning of this course that very few people fail. So my interest is more in whether I have done well enough to be awarded a merit, and of that I am less optimistic. I suspect these are handed out more sparingly, and in view of my poor mark in my 'Teaching Creative Writing' essay (only 55%) I think I may have spoilt my chances. Still, a pass will suffice. I can't help thinking I have done pretty well to complete the course at all, given the extraordinary circumstances pertaining throughout. I intend to be there on the awards day as well, lining up with all the young people in my gown and mortar board. When I accepted my medical degree in 1974 it was presented by David Attenborough, no less, who was there to receive an honorary DSc for his 'Outstanding contribution to the popularising of science'. And that was *before* his celebrated *Life on Earth* television series secured him worldwide iconic status. I hardly think such an eminent personage will be handing out the degrees on this occasion. I'll be lucky if I get Ant or Dec. No matter, I'm getting that degree, and I'm going to frame it and put it up on the wall too.

Chapter Seventeen

This place is a little paradise
– Karl Marx

It is Sunday the first of October 2017, three pm. I am sitting on the observation deck of the "Red Osprey" car ferry as it makes its way up Southampton Water from East Cowes on the Isle of Wight.

I am reading Gay Talese's marvellous essay on the *New York Times* chief obituary writer, Alden Whitman, entitled *Mr Bad News*, written in 1966. Every few paragraphs I lift my eyes from the print to watch the profusion of traffic on this, one of the busiest waterways in the world. There are many yachts, some travelling in the same direction as ourselves. One by one, we slowly overhaul them, though I imagine with a favourable wind they could keep up or even overtake us. Then the sedate atmosphere is shattered by twenty or so jet skis which seem to come out of nowhere, bearing down on us like a gang of marauding pirates. They buzz around us like angry bees, coming so close we can hear the whoops of delight from their drivers as they zip past just yards from our hull. They bounce around so alarmingly it seems at any moment they will be pitched into the sea, but they must hold on to their handlebars with an iron grip, for no one goes flying into the drink.

We had decided to visit the Isle of Wight in part as a kind of compare-and-contrast exercise with the Isle of Man, which we visited two months ago. And the contrasts are plain to see. The Isle of Man seems a very separate part of the United Kingdom; everywhere you go you can feel its fierce sense of autonomy from the mainland. In Manx, it even claims its own language.

The Isle of Wight, on the other hand, represents the very heart of little England. Both culturally and topographically, it feels as if a one hundred and fifty square mile rhombus of the

Hampshire coast had simply fallen into the sea and come to rest a few miles offshore. Unlike the Isle of Man, the Romans did land here. Julius Caesar named the island *Vectis*, and although no garrison was ever stationed here, a couple of roads were built, and the remains of seven luxurious villas have been found.

When we travelled out on Thursday it was mild, though there was a fine rain, so familiar to us in South Wales, but by the time we reached Ventnor on its southern coast, the sun had come out and the little town was bathed in golden, late afternoon sunshine.

Ventnor is said to enjoy a microclimate, protected from the elements by snuggling up against the imposing rump of St Boniface Down, much as Great Malvern shelters from the weather by cozying up to the flanks of the Malvern Hills. It was Sir William Gull,[35] personal physician to Queen Victoria, who first noted the healing properties of the air here, and a vogue began for building sanatoria to treat the middle classes of Victorian England for their chronic lung conditions; consumption, emphysema and especially asthma. And it is for this reason I have decided to base my stay on the Isle of Wight in Ventnor, because it was here, in 1959, that I was sent for control of my own asthma, to a school specialising in the treatment of that condition, and other 'delicate children'.

Once settled into our hotel room, our first excursion was to this establishment, still extant after its founding in 1895, though it now focuses more on children with ADHD and those on the autistic spectrum. A walk of only a few hundred yards finds us outside its entrance, the stone lintel above its imposing oak door carved with the words:

ST CATHERINE'S HOME

St Catherine's *Home*. Not so much a *school*, then, as a *home*. And it *was* a home for me, for nearly two years, until my asthma was considered sufficiently improved to render me eligible for release. Of course asthma tends to improve spontaneously as children reach double figures, so that factor may have been as important as the health-giving effects of the air.

Expecting the proprietors to be less than anxious to admit even an old boy to a working school, which in any event had

---

35 Interestingly, he later became a potential candidate for being Jack the Ripper. Nothing came of it of course. The Ripper remains unidentified to this day.

probably changed out of all recognition since my day, we decided not to attempt to gain entrance. But we did crane our necks over its walls to look at its playing fields, and there was the football pitch, just as I remembered it, cut down to half-size as a concession to the compromised lung function of the players.

Looming above the school is St Boniface Down, which from time to time the entire school would be made to climb, coughing and wheezing and spluttering their way up to the Trig point which stands at 239 metres above sea level. No one was excused the outing, except those so incapacitated they were confined to the school's infirmary. Everyone else had to go, teachers, cooks, cleaners, all led by the formidable figure of Sister Kathleen, matron and spiritual leader of this deeply religious institution. Very high church, I remember being almost intoxicated by the smell of incense in the chapel, which still stands in its grounds. That was part of my 'religious phase', when for a time I considered a career in the priesthood. That is until my mid-teens, when logic won out over faith.

Of course not all the children had trouble gaining the heights. Some almost bounded up the hill, laughing at their fellows struggling far below them. Asthma is a strange condition. In a full-on attack the sufferer is scarcely able to breathe, especially on the out-breath. It becomes difficult to expel air from the lungs, and in childhood the chest often develops the classical 'barrel-shaped' deformity because of over-inflation. In remissions, however, there is no dyspnoea at all. In 1976, the great Scottish swimmer David Wilkie, an asthma sufferer, won the 200 metres breaststroke gold at the Montreal Olympics. Clearly he was not in difficulties that day. Had he been, he would have been forced to stay in his room and watch the event on television.

The following day we re-traced the steps of my childhood. Although less than five hundred metres from the sea, St Catherine's is one hundred metres above it; making one's way from any location to another in Ventnor always seems to involve negotiating a steep hill. From the school, it is another one hundred and forty metres up a vertiginous pull until one is through the woods, past the bramble strewn steps cut into the hill and out onto the downs.

Even from the heights of St Boniface Down, the coast of

France, more than two hundred miles distant, lies well beyond the horizon, hidden behind the curvature of the Earth. Despite that, some locals still claim to have seen it, though, they say, some trick of the light renders the image upside down.

More easily visible on the western horizon is nearby Brighstone Forest, destination for another regular mass outing from the school. Twice a year in the summer months the entire school would travel there in a small convoy of coaches and play a game of hide and seek, half the pupils hiding and the other half seeking them. I hated it. I was lousy at hiding and never seemed to be able to find anyone. And it was on one of these occasions I experienced what I now think was my own case of child sexual abuse.

I was trudging to the edge of the woods, intending to wait there until everyone had been found and we could all go home, when I was spotted by a teacher.

"What are you doing, boy? Why aren't you taking part?"

I started to explain that I wasn't feeling very well and was going to go on to say I thought I might be allergic to some of the trees, but he didn't give me the chance.

"I know what's going on here. You don't like this game and you've opted out. You know perfectly well that participation is compulsory, so you know you're breaking the rules. I'm afraid you'll have to be punished. Take your trousers down. And your pants."

"But Sir?"

"Don't argue with me, child. Do as you are told. At once!"

Having no option, I lowered my clothes and adopted the position. Mr P, a very tall, very angular man with pale blue eyes and a permanent five o'clock shadow, sat on a tree trunk as I laid myself across his lap. I remember noticing, and not for the first time, how bony his knees were. He drew his hand back and gave me a single, hard slap across the buttocks. In the quiet of the forest the sound of it rang out like a rifle shot. His hand remained there for one, two seconds.

"You may put your trousers back on. There, now that wasn't too bad, was it?"

His demeanour changed from hostile to kind in a moment. He ruffled my hair, put his arm round my shoulder and invited me to join him in the seekers party, where we enjoyed great success. As we walked he told me some of the secrets of the game, such as stopping every few minutes and standing in silence, waiting for the hiders to betray themselves by making a sound.

The fact was that Mr P was a popular teacher. We put up with his style of corporal punishment because to us, even though we were quite often subjected to these slaps, it was far less harsh than the beatings some of the other teachers inflicted. Some would use the cane (though not on bare buttocks), or worse, make us write out one hundred lines, such as:

I must stop looking out of the window during class and pay more attention, lest I fall behind in my studies.

Note the line is carefully designed to be long enough to extend to the line below, making the copying process even more awkward.

I was not the only boy who noticed how Mr P curiously changed from foe to friend the moment the punishment had been delivered, but never did it occur to any of us that we were being sexually exploited. And certainly, compared to the kind of things I have been accused of, it scarcely registers on the radar. I don't think it warped me, or any of the other boys who experienced it, though it is interesting that I still remember it, despite an interim of nearly sixty years.

Although my most venerable psychosomatic condition, asthma, was relatively well controlled during my brief sojourn on the Isle of Wight, there were plenty of others to keep me going. Most notable among them was a stiffness in the hips and knees, which began to intensify not long after my return from the Isle of Man. My friend Owen refers to such things as 'age accelerants', and it seems an appropriate term. There is no doubt that it makes me *feel*, and indeed *look*, like a much older man. After even the briefest periods of inactivity, such as sitting in a car or relaxing in an armchair, it is as if my joints have completely seized, and I find myself barely able to walk, shoulders hunched forward like someone escaping from an old people's home. Thankfully, walking any distance diminishes the tightness a little, though a dull awareness persists, even in bed, where I have found myself waking in discomfort several times each night. Then all my problems come back to me and I have to face the challenge of putting them to one side and getting back to sleep again. High-dose paracetamol eases the pain to some extent, which is a sign there is nothing truly serious at the root of it, but one cannot take pain-killers indefinitely: even paracetamol can be dangerous if the recommended dose is exceeded.

This is not entirely new: a couple of years ago, when I was still working, I first became aware of a problem in my hips and arranged an X-ray. It showed only minimal degenerative change, 'in keeping with the age of the patient', the report stated. A sobering thought. But the knee problem *is* new. I probably have minor arthritis there too, but there can be no doubting the underlying cause. The same can be said for my low back pain and stiff neck, both of which problems have a far older vintage. These have been recurrent problems for me since my twenties, and throughout our four days on the 'South island' (residents of the Isle of Wight refer to the mainland as 'North Island'), they were waiting to come at me and spoil any experience, however pleasurable or diverting it might be.

They were there when we marvelled at the Isle of Wight's most iconic landmark, The Needles. As we approached them we were treated to the sight of a World War Two Spitfire overhead, diving and weaving around a more slowly moving helicopter, from which I presume it was being filmed. It reminded me of the time I once saw a hapless buzzard being mobbed by a crow. But today, even looking up was uncomfortable.

They didn't go away when we wandered round Carisbrooke Castle, thirteenth century fortress home to Isabella de Fortibus, much beloved 'Queen of Wight', and sole owner of the island.[36] Walking around the castle's impressive and lengthy curtain walls, perhaps following in Isabella's own footsteps, was for me one long, uncomfortable chore.

And they persisted even on our last day on the island, a day of glorious Indian summer radiance. As we surveyed the grand, gutted shell of Appuldurcombe House, reduced to ruins by an errant German land mine in 1943, the tightness in my joints, if

---

36 But Edward Longshanks coveted her property, and in 1293, on her deathbed, he pressured her into selling up for the derisory sum of 6,000 marks.

not my concerns for the future, dogged my every step. But it could have been worse. At least I didn't lose my camera.

*

Monday the sixteenth of October 2017, eleven am. I am just back from Merthyr Tydfil, doing a small favour for a friend who doesn't drive. Still trying desperately to live a 'normal' life, which meant, as far as this particular friend was concerned, pretending nothing at all was wrong in my life. As we approached the town, it became so murky overhead the streetlights came on, and I found it necessary to use my headlights. Other than during a total solar eclipse, I have never seen the skies so dark when it should have been broad daylight. Then, as we were driving back into Cardiff, my friend said something about 'a red Sun'. I was busy concentrating on the road at the time, and didn't really pay attention to her odd remark. But when I got out of the car, I saw it for myself: its outline clear behind the now thinning cloud, the Sun was indeed a deep magenta red, and later I noticed its radiance permeating into every room. As time passed it changed to an orange hue, and stayed that way for several hours before reverting to its customary yellow-white brilliance.

Later I discovered the reason for these strange, and for me, unique, phenomena. Apparently the hurricane formerly known as Ophelia, taking an unusual north-easterly path across the Atlantic, swept up a huge plume of Saharan dust and carried it towards the British Isles. And as it passed over Portugal, it may also have collected clouds of ash rising from massive forest fires raging in its interior.

As someone who has been fascinated by atmospheric phenomena since childhood, seeing this very rare phenomenon should have been a marvellous, even ecstatic experience for me. But the truth was that almost all of the joy was sucked out of it, nullified by the underlying sense of dread I feel at almost every waking moment. Whether it be a rainbow, a sundog or even a murmuration of starlings, it is always the same: the fear overlays everything. Will I ever again be in a position to appreciate the beauty of the world like other people? Perhaps, I think sometimes, this will be my life forever.

★

Mark Crowley today almost purrs with satisfaction as he relates some interesting revelations uncovered by Simon C's barrister. His mood is infectious, but only for a moment.

"This is excellent news, Stephen. Very encouraging."

"You mean they might drop the case now?"

"Sadly no."

Suddenly my ebullience is deflated.

"True, it casts doubt on the reliability of Florence's testimony, and every time we can do this it chips away at their case. But no, it is not so devastating to the prosecution that they will abandon their case. They've invested far too much time and energy into putting you and the others behind bars for them to stop now. We need more. A lot more. But it *is* good news."

Walking back from my solicitor's office on what has now turned into a fine autumn evening, the stiffness in my neck, hips and knees continues undiminished, despite today's positive news. But I am not so naïve as to think it might all go away the moment I hear a bit of good news. Stress isn't like that. Even after February of next year, when with any luck I will find myself a free man, I can expect these symptoms to persist for months. The body learns patterns of behaviour which it does not relinquish easily. I remember a Tibetan Buddhist guru once putting it this way:

"The mind learns fast and forgets fast. The body learns slow but remembers."

Tantalisingly, about a week ago I was watching the television when I suddenly became aware that all my tension had melted away. I started dancing around the room in joy, flaunting my freedom of movement to my astonished and delighted wife. But it didn't last. The following morning I awoke as tightly knotted as ever. I can only hope that when I am called to the stand the adrenaline surge will temporarily overwhelm the stiffness. I don't want the jury to see me hobbling in court like an arthritic old man. They might think I was trying to prey on their sympathy.

★

Wednesday the twenty-fifth of October 2017, nine-thirty am. Another development. I am at Cardiff Bay police station, having been *requested*, rather than *required* to attend by the police, in order to collect my seized items. I have Owen to thank for this.

When he was not 'harassing' Cath Orford with complaining emails, Owen had been spending a lot of time online researching similar cases to our own. Partly because his wife's computer had been seized as well as his own, the latter containing important data relating to her work, he had looked into the law regarding seizures. He found the following in PACE:

"If the seized material may easily be copied, then the property should be returned *within a reasonable time period.*"

Obviously the police are not going to return a gun, a knife or a piece of bloody clothing, but computer files and photographs *can* be copied easily, and therefore *should* be returned. Despite this the police rarely return property before trial, and often delay giving it back for months even when the accused is found not guilty, and never if they are convicted. Owen fired off a series of emails at them, quoting the law and demanding his property be returned. They stalled for months, giving one lame excuse after another,[37] but then, to everyone's amazement, two weeks ago they released them. This prompted me to get my solicitors on the case to get my property returned. Within days the reply came back: I could come down and retrieve them at my convenience.

I didn't realise how much the police had taken from my house. Apart from my two computers and address book, they had seized nearly fifteen hundred holiday snaps taken over a thirty year period: group shots of the family at Strumble Head, at the Pentre Ifan burial chamber, at the castle of Carreg Cennen, at Tintern Abbey, on the beach in Tenerife, Crete and a host of other sunny locations; the list is almost endless. Unfortunately for them, however, nothing in any way incriminating. In particular, none of Florence posing semi-naked, despite her claims that such photos had indeed been taken on several occasions. I almost pitied them going through them all. Almost. But what I found most remarkable was the attitude of the police. Far from their usual demeanour of cold hostility, they were all smiles, and the whole atmosphere was as if they were

---

37 One was that a relevant police officer was 'off sick' – for several months.

pleased to be returning some valuable item of lost property.

Liz had warned me to check the condition of my equipment before taking it away. She had heard computers are sometimes returned with their screens smashed, so I was ready with my camera to photograph them, right there in the police station, just in case. I opened my two laptops, but they were undamaged. The police then loaded the whole lot into a huge plastic bag, before obligingly carrying it out to my car and loading it into the boot for me. I half expected them to wave goodbye.

Later, to my utter amazement, we discovered that the computers were never examined. The police had delivered them to the regional 'High-Tech Crime Unit', but when the latter learned the details of the case, they decided that as all the alleged crimes had been committed more than twenty years ago, they would be unlikely to find anything of evidentiary value. And despite repeated pleas from the police and, indeed, the CPS to change their minds, their view prevailed. I have to say I find this astonishing. The police are saying all the defendants are paedophiles. In which case it is highly likely we would have collections of child porn on our computers. Owen has told me that nearly every convicted paedophile is found to have downloaded thousands of images of child pornographers onto their laptops. And if even one such image had been found on our devices, it would have been a hammer-blow to our defence. Yet they never even looked!

This was wonderful news for me. None of the potentially embarrassing material on my computer would be produced at trial. I began to feel a little better. But only a little. The police, and of course the CPS, still knew that I, a doctor, counted a disreputable man among his friends, a man who had gone into hiding, perhaps to avoid the consequences of his horrible crimes. And I knew they were still ferreting away to find any more dirt on me that might be out there...

Meanwhile in America the Harvey Weinstein scandal has broken and the *Me Too* campaign has captured the public's imagination around the world. From now on, it seems, there is to be zero tolerance for sexual harassment, and a good thing too. But I worry about how all this will impact on the minds of any given jury. Our alleged offences fall far outside the zone of mere harassment, so perhaps I am worrying over nothing. As someone who has never sexually harassed a woman in his entire life, let alone raped and tortured them, I support the *Me Too* and *Time's Up!* campaigns one hundred per cent. But at this moment I am in such a state of tension that the slightest thing can put me into a panic.

Chapter Eighteen

The waiting is the hardest part
– Tom Petty

Thursday the ninth of November 2017, two am. A man without a face hands me a telephone.

"I have the complainant on the line now, sir. Here she is."

"Hello, Florence, is that you?"

"Yes."

"Florence, why did you say those things about me? When you knew I did nothing to hurt you? Hello? Are you there?"

Silence.

I wake up.

Often in the midst of a crisis we do not dream about the issue which is troubling us most. But if the crisis is sufficiently long-lasting, we do. I now find myself dreaming about my problem, in one form or another, almost every night. Apparently, and I say apparently because I have no memory of it, a couple of weeks ago my wife was woken by my snoring. According to her, I proceeded to sit bolt upright, and then, speaking loudly and clearly, I cried:

"Not guilty!"

I then lay down and resumed my snoring.

A few nights later I dream I am free-climbing a vertical sea-stack, a little like the Old Man of Hoy. I am holding on by my fingertips; hundreds of feet below I can hear the seas boiling, see giant breakers crashing against the rocks. A strong updraft is coming at me up the vertical face, tousling my hair and threatening my already precarious position. There is a smell of ozone on the wind. It seems I am about to fall, but then the thought occurs: *you're not going to fall.* I let go. Nothing happens. I do not fall, but hang there, floating in space. In the few moments before

I wake from the dream, I am filled with an ineffable sense of joy. When I awake, I think, a joyful dream? Now?

It is Friday the seventeenth of November 2017, eleven am. The weather is fine but cold; there was a ground frost last night, a rare thing for Cardiff in November.

November seventeenth is a date I have been looking forward to for a long time. I should be standing in the dock with my four co-accused, listening to the lawyers arguing their separate cases in the 'PTR' (Pre-Trial Review). But I am not. I am sitting at home, writing this. Yesterday afternoon I got a call from my solicitor saying it had been called off at the last moment, re-scheduled for a week hence. Our trial judge, Tom Crowther, QC, has been delayed by other commitments and is unable to be in court today. But perhaps it is no bad thing.

Two weeks ago a second round of unused materials was released by the prosecution at the defence's insistence, but because my team had been doing all the lobbying it was only released to us. Finally, two days ago, it was released to the others as well. This vast tranche of documents will take some time for the other lawyers to trawl through. I myself have spent days on this very task, in particular reading the five hundred and thirty-three emails that have been exchanged between my accuser and DC Cath Orford, in the course of just one year.[38] We have already seen a few of these emails, but this new batch confirms the extraordinary relationship the two have developed in the five years the investigation has dragged on. What is not contained in the disclosures is any of the doubtless numerous text messages that must have passed between them, or any records of phone calls. Police officers should log every call they make connected to a case, and note its content. My team will be demanding these too be released for our scrutiny. But what we have already covers hundreds of pages of text, and every one has this little comment attached:

"Of no value to the prosecution and therefore may be of value to the defence"

---

38 They run between July of last year to this July and then peter out.

These emails make for extremely disconcerting reading. In a separate bundle of documents entitled 'Officer's Reports', Cath Orford attempts to explain what struck me as a very strange relationship with the complainant. She reports that attempts were made early on to assign a 'Family Liaison Officer' to Florence, whose job would be to provide 'pastoral support', but none was available. Such a move would in any event have been highly unusual, because their use is generally restricted to helping the families of murder victims or kidnapped children. In the event Cath Orford reluctantly took it upon herself to take on the joint tasks of 'OIC' (Officer In the Case) *and* unofficial FLO. Whether she had approval from higher up the chain of command for this decision is not clear, though in the enormous welter of information I am tasked with trawling through, I could have missed it.[39]

In another folder are emails exchanges between police officers researching my son's death. They knew he had died suddenly in August 2006, and it now emerges they had convinced themselves he had committed suicide, perhaps as a result of the abuse I had supposedly inflicted on him over the years. You can sense the disappointment in their exchanges when they find the report from his inquest, where the coroner determined his cause of death as:

'Natural causes; specific cause unknown'

As I read these notes I feel physically sick. That they would stoop so low as to trash the reputation of my boy in their bid to take me down is unendurable. I have to stop reading, breathing hard, my eyes filling with tears.

My legal team, however, are exultant at the revelations about the police's handling of the case. If the lead investigating officer has been conflating two very separate roles, it could taint the whole investigation. Their plan is to demand Cath Orford be removed from the case,[40] and this is one of the points that would have been thrashed out this morning. Even if that fails, she can be guaranteed an extremely uncomfortable time on the witness stand when the time comes for her to give evidence. But we will

39 Later I scanned the materials again and found she had indeed obtained permission from her DCI.
40 It never happened. She continued working on the case to its conclusion.

have to wait until next week to see how the argument develops.

*

My list of stress-related ailments continues to grow. The tightness in my limbs and joints has now spread to my shoulder girdle. In the last few weeks I have noticed my upper arms and shoulders becoming increasingly limited in their range of movement. It is not that I cannot move my arms. It is just that I get a little jolt of pain every time I do.

I have long been a supporter of psychodynamics, a simple model for understanding human motivation and behaviour. Why we do what we do; why we suffer the things we suffer, has been a source of fascination for me since my earliest days as a doctor. And I have formed a hypothesis for my current problems which goes a little further than simply saying 'It's all down to stress'. I now believe my body has made a kind of pact with fate: if I suffer now, it will indemnify me against possible future disaster. It would be wrong to sail through this crisis without any kind of glitch, a sin against *karma* if you will. I suffer now, so that I will be all right later. My wife, also a student of psychodynamics, offers a simpler explanation: "You're doing everything you can to hold yourself together; you're just holding yourself together *too tightly.*"

So I try not to feel too sorry for myself. It could be a lot worse. My back has not seized up for some time, my alimentary system has not let me down, and I haven't had a full-blown panic attack for months. Perhaps most importantly of all, I am getting enough sleep. And I am still writing.

Wednesday the twenty-second of November, 2017, nine-thirty am. Just over two months to go before my trial begins. I am outside my solicitor's office, but it is closed. Instead of the usual hive of activity inside, the staff are milling about outside like so many lost sheep. It seems there has been a local power-cut, and the electronic keypad used to unlock the door is not working. I will have to come back later.

Two hours later and they have gained access. I go inside and they give me a new disc, on which are scrawled in felt-tip pen the words *CPS Disclosures Phase 3*. There is too much information on it to send in an email. Even this huge document does not represent *all* of the information my defence team has demanded, and that the CPS has agreed to provide. In court on Friday the defence will complain to the judge about the CPS's continuing procrastination; then finally, some time in December, we may get it all.

There are more emails between Florence and Cath Orford on the disc, but the bulk of it is transcripts of over one thousand text messages. In a one year period, a day rarely passes without at least two or three being sent; on some days the figure exceeds thirty. I settle down and start reading. An hour passes, two, three. In the event I spend over six hours going through all the messages, taking notes as I go.

What did I find? A quick summary might be: 'more of the same'. More of Florence complaining about how cruel life is to her and what a strain it is knowing she will have to appear in court and repeat her story in front of strangers. And more of Cath supporting her emotionally every step of the way; reassuring, ego-reinforcing, stroking, indeed, everything a good counsellor should be doing. Though she presumably has received no training for the additional role she has adopted, one has to say she has done a pretty good job of it. Of course it is easy to understand why: should Florence pull the plug, the case falls to the ground. She *has* to stay on board. And in the margins of the printout, as before, every text message is appended with the comment about them holding no value to the prosecution's case, hence possibly being of assistance to the defence. The rules of Contempt of Court once again preclude me from quoting any of the texts verbatim, which in a way is no bad thing. If I quoted them all this book would run to over a thousand pages. But I will say this. DC Oxford was clearly totally committed to her work as unofficial family liaison officer, willing to email, text message or phone her 'client' day and night, seven days a week.

After hours of trawling through the exchanges, I experience what alcoholics sometimes refer to as 'a moment of clarity'. I wonder why it hadn't occurred to me before: Cath Orford is being *groomed* by Florence. And whether she is aware of it or not, Cath is participating avidly. Acting more or less as an unpaid counsellor, the exchanges between them, to my eye at least, carry a remarkably similar flavour to those we have seen between Florence and her therapist.

Other emails between the police officers show that Florence has already received substantial compensation from CICA (the Criminal Injuries Compensation Authority) for 'alleged sexual abuse', following a claim lodged by Florence within weeks of her original round of interviews in 2013. It seems Cath Orford is now assisting Florence in preparing a fresh claim in light of the more recent charges.

Here at last we find the statements from her brother and sister, but they add little of substantive value.

*

Friday the twenty-fourth of November 2017, ten am. I am in Courtroom Three at Cardiff Crown Court. For some reason I find myself thinking about apples. In the last few days we have been collecting the last of this year's bumper crop, prior to my wife baking them into apple sauce. This will then be used to enhance our breakfasts, stirred into my yoghurt or her porridge.

My brief reverie is broken when Judge Tom Crowther, QC, enters the courtroom and we are admonished to stand in respect. He takes his seat, and we are allowed to resume ours. Cushions have been placed on the bench for our comfort, but behind our backs there is only an unforgiving brass rail. I remind myself, as this is the courtroom that will be used in the actual trial, that I am going to need an extra cushion if I am to sit here, hour after hour, in anything approaching comfort. A reporter sits in his place close to the judge, taking notes and occasionally glancing at us. I am in the dock with my four co-accused. I am on the far right, as I am number one on the indictment sheet.

On my immediate left is Eric E, facing eleven charges, more or less the same as mine, with the exception of the abortion charge and the one where she claims I groped her when she was unwell. To his left his brother Michael, facing three serious charges, though not rape. Then comes Simon, who faces six similar charges, and finally, at the other end of the bench, my friend Owen, who faces only two.

The first order of the day is to have each of our charges read out to us and plead 'guilty' or 'not guilty'. It occurs to me the judge could simply have asked if any of us wished to change our pleas from last time; we could each have said "no", which would have taken about a minute and we could have moved on. But no, we have to sit (the judge has advised us that we may remain seated through this part of the proceedings) as the clerk of the court reads out the charges, one by one, waiting for the right moment to say: "Not guilty!"

I say the words as clearly and assertively as I can. But just like the last time, I feel an intense sense of unreality as again and again I say the words. This can't be *me* they're talking about, can it? Am I doing this on behalf of someone else perhaps? I wonder if the others are feeling the same. Eric E sounds exhausted as he protests his innocence. His brother Michael sounds almost bored. Owen's words seem to drip with contempt at the whole process. Only Simon puts real emotion into his words, which are uttered with a palpable sense of anger. Eventually, after nearly twenty-five minutes, the job is done and the business of the day can begin.

We are represented by our wig-wearing barristers, eight in all. Several members of the various solicitor's teams are also in court, though they of course are wig-less. My leading counsel, Christopher Clee, QC, opens the batting on my behalf as is only fitting, as his client will be tried first. Fortunately the acoustics in the courtroom are good and I can hear every word, notwithstanding my tinnitus, which at this moment is screaming.

He starts to talk about 'Section 8', whatever that is.[41] The exchanges are so arcane no non-lawyer would have a ghost of a chance understanding what is going on; even today, when the use of Latin and Greek phrases have been barred from the courtroom. But then I suppose doctors discussing a complex case would sound just as confusing to an outsider. Slowly, things begin to become a little clearer. My counsel goes on to discuss the way DC Cath Orford has been communicating with the 'complainant'.

---

41 I found out later this was Section 8 of the Criminal Procedure and Investigation Act, 1996, which allows the defence to challenge the CPS over any perceived failure in their duty of disclosure of materials likely to be beneficial to the defence.

"Your Honour has not seen the unused materials yet; I understand that, but he needs to be aware of the 533 emails, over 1,000 text messages and 118 phone calls exchanged between Ms Orford and the complainant in the last year alone. And that despite regulations, none of the contents of the phone calls have been logged."

"You are right to say I have not had sight of the Unused Materials, Mr Clee. There will be ample opportunity to discuss these later, of course, though I dare say this is not going to be the last time we hear those statistics trotted out in this court."

The judge is not wrong. We hear them quoted again just one minute later when the second defence barrister gets to his feet.

"See?" says the judge. "Told you."

The defence are told to prepare a 'skeleton argument' which will be pursued regarding Section 8.

"Remember, gentlemen, Section 8 is a very powerful tool", the judge says.

Alongside the Section 8 argument, the defence will be massing forces to highlight the 'Abuse of Process', while the prosecution prepares their rebuttal, though it is hard to see how they will defend the police's actions. We have now all seen the huge tranche of communications referred to above, and soon the judge too will have sight of them. Arguments about 'Section 8' and 'Abuse of Process' will take place on the first day of the trial proper, which Judge Crowther confirms is likely to last four weeks. Then the proceedings are concluded and the accused are allowed to leave.

My counsel calls me into a side room adjacent to the court to discuss the issues. For the first time he tells me he feels 'confident' about securing an acquittal for me, which comes as a huge relief. I'd have preferred 'supremely confident', or even 'very confident', but 'confident' will have to suffice. I imagine it is as far as he ever goes in predicting the outcome of a trial.

I resume my mental rehearsal for how to cope with being attacked on the stand about my character, something I have been doing almost without a break since July of last year. Chris Clee agrees to give me some help in how to deal to it, "closer to the trial date".

Outside the court, a film cameraman and another man with a phone follow my progress towards our car. The weather is fine and sunny; in truth a beautiful day in late autumn. I walk briskly but steadily, head held high, studiously ignoring the photographers. Liz is by my side. Owen, who has left his wife at home, accompanies us. Finally, after about sixty metres, the press leaves us alone. My only concession to disguise, a Panama hat, pulled well down. On the way home in the car, Liz says:

"I've got to say it: being chased down the street by a reporter from the BBC because my husband had been accused of terrible sex crimes is one of the things I never thought would happen to me."

Me neither.

Later the story is referred to briefly on the BBC local news, with film of me shown leaving the court. Of the five accused, only my name is mentioned.

"Dr Stephen Glascoe, seen here in the white hat, and four other men are accused of a variety of sexual offences against young girls [sic]..."

That seems a trifle unfair, but I am scarcely in a position to complain. And it is true; I do make by far the best copy, especially with the "miscarriage" charge, as the BBC described it. So the story is now in the public domain. The guardian angel who has protected us so far has flown away, as we knew he would eventually. At least we have had five months of grace since our court appearance on the sixteenth of June. Better to be grateful for small mercies, than dwell on the grim reality that everyone who knows my name now knows I am charged with terrible crimes against a young girl, or 'girls' as the BBC stated. I miss the broadcast myself, but the following day a friend phones to report the fact that it made it to the BBC Wales news at both six-thirty and ten-thirty pm.

"Was it easy to recognise me?"

"Nah. You were just some bloke in a white hat. Couldn't really see your face. We don't usually watch the local news, but it came on right before Graham Norton, which is why we caught it."

As for other news outlets, I have found nothing.[42] Perhaps there is a degree of 'media fatigue' surrounding historical sexual abuse.

---

42 Later I discovered that it had been reported, in Welsh, on the BBC Cymru website, with all the defendants named.

*

Saturday the ninth of December 2017, six-thirty am. Why so early? I am just back from from town, where I dropped Liz off at the train station. She is London bound, to attend a conference entitled: 'EXPLAINING THE SPIRITUAL IN MUSIC' One of the presentations that caught her eye is called: '*Music and the Hidden World – the role of music in the healing rituals of the Wana people of central Sulawesi*'.

When I spotted this item on the programme I remarked that I wouldn't mind going to that myself, but she pointed out that the conference is not open to the public, adding: "I've been to these sorts of things before, and trust me, they aren't half as interesting as you might think."

Nonetheless, I look forward to hearing her report of proceedings. Meanwhile, the cats are lobbying for their breakfast, but it is too early. My tortoiseshell, Matilda, has positioned herself directly behind my laptop, from where she stares fixedly at me. My ginger tom, Rufus, sits atop the microwave, tapping me lightly on the arm each time I walk past. At first his claws are retracted, but then he uses them, pulling strands from my jumper. I take the hint and give them their morning pouch.

Yesterday was the deadline for yet another bolus of disclosures to be released to the defence by the CPS, as per the judge's orders. But I have heard nothing yet from my lawyers, so I can only assume they are late yet again, as they have been throughout this whole sorry process. As part of his coping strategy, Owen has been researching other cases of false allegations, and he tells me this sort of deliberate time-wasting on the part of the CPS is very much standard practice.

"You know, I don't know where you find the strength to delve into all these other cases. I'd just find it all too upsetting," I said to him.

"For me it's a kind of therapy, I guess, like when I was having a go at Cath Orford. But then there's you with your writing. I don't know how you can do *that*. How do you do it, by the way?"

"I suppose that's *my* therapy. I guess we've all developed our own different mechanisms. I wonder how the others are coping."

There is a brief silence as we consider the question. Although the ban on the defendants contacting one another has been lifted, neither of us has even thought of trying to get in touch with them. What would we say?

"So, we're in seriously deep shit here, right?"

"Oh God aye. Do you think we're going to be alright?"

"I dunno. From where I'm standing it could go either way. Put it another way, I'm shitting myself right now."

"Me too."

(Embarrassed silence)

"So, anyway, good luck."

"Yeah, same to you mate. See you in court, right?"

"I guess."

I'd like to ask them, in view of their insistence they had never met her, how Florence came to pick on them, but this wouldn't be the right time to ask. In my mind there can only be one conclusion: there must be a question of mistaken identity going on here. Yet another E brother, Kevin, *did* know Ken D, Florence's dad; apparently *was* present at several of those notorious parties. Did Florence mix them up somehow? I feel sure that's what they'd say, though we may never learn the full truth of this. I am sure of only one thing: they are no more guilty than I am.

Two weeks on from my last court appearance, I am in another of those strange periods of limbo where nothing is happening and I can almost pretend life is normal. In reality of course, that is impossible. In a little over seven weeks I am due to stand trial charged with committing a series of horrific crimes against a young girl, my fate resting on the decision of twelve people I have never met.

This morning there was a thick layer of frost on the car. Winter is here, and Christmas is at hand. A huge cell of polar air has drifted down from the Arctic, and snow is lying in many parts of Wales, though Cardiff, as so often happens, is spared. There were a few desultory snowflakes yesterday, falling out of an apparently empty sky, but it failed to amount to anything. Fortunately for her, I have just had a text from Liz saying the train is *en route,* its progress unimpeded by ice on the line, or worse, 'the wrong kind of snow'.

We are attempting to lead a 'normal life', though it is proving a challenge. Two weeks ago, just two days before I was due to appear in Courtroom Number Three, my car was captured by a mobile speed camera, doing thirty-five in a thirty zone. Then, five days later, in a different location entirely, Liz was caught doing the same thing. Coincidence? Of course not. My last speeding ticket being fifteen years ago, I have been offered a place on a 'speed awareness course', which avoids points on my license, though the cost of attending it is the same as the fine I would have incurred. Unfortunately, Liz's last offence was more recent, so she will have to take the points.

But it is not all bad news. About ten days ago I checked my university email account, to find I have been formally awarded my MA – with a merit! I was beside myself with joy for about ten seconds before I started to think, how many merits did they award? Presumably they don't hand them out on a whim, but there were at least three, maybe more, writers on the course who were at least as good as me and perhaps better. I doubt if any were awarded a distinction, though I cannot say for sure. There is no easy way to find out beyond asking my professor, and I am not about to do that. So I shall be content with my achievement, happy and really quite amazed that I have done it all despite the ominous shadow hanging over my life.

Of the nine pieces I submitted in my two writing portfolios, three were deemed by the examiners to be 'of publishable quality', a term I believe they use sparingly. The first, *A Quiet Day*, forms the prologue to this book. The second, a fictional short story called *Intelligent Fingers*, concerns a man who wakes one morning to find his hands have mysteriously disappeared. Once liberated from their body, the hands acquire extraordinary skills in the fields of both music and writing, though it soon emerges that they are also engaging in acts which their owner, a staid and respectable magistrate, would never dream of committing, except perhaps in the darkest recesses of his subconscious. The third piece, which received the most unanimous approval of all my submissions, was called *A House in Cardiff*.

In this story, in which I drew inspiration from French writer Georges Perec's masterpiece *Life A Users Manual*, I offer a detailed description of my own house,[43] along with thumbnail portraits of its two occupants. I found it surprisingly easy to write, and was even more surprised by the amount of praise it received. It was one of those rare occasions, familiar to all writers, when I found the story 'writing itself'. I offer this brief extract, which goes some way to explaining my mindset at the time I wrote it, almost exactly a year ago:

"...*Work in the garden is divided along unchanging, if unstated, guidelines. The man tends to the lawn, mowing, edging, feeding, while the woman looks after the flowerbeds and does the pruning. This work appears to have been a little neglected recently.*

The man of the house lets his gaze wander around the kitchen. In the low winter sun, isolated pockets of accumulated dust and grime catch his eye, lurking in corners unnoticed in the summer months. Occasionally one of the householders will attack these little islands with gusto, eliminating a few of them. But a process like this requires energy, and this commodity has been in short supply of late..."

I fear those pockets of dust are still there...

To provide an escape, albeit temporarily, from my problems, I continue to watch old movies that hold a special place in my heart: *The Searchers, Dr Strangelove, The Man in the White Suit*; movies I must have seen dozens of times in the course of my life. But I have seen a few films for the first time this year which have also afforded enormous pleasure; notably Antonioni's devastating takedown of Rome's *glitterati, La Notte*, Jacques Becker's wickedly subversive *Casque D'Or*, the film which heralded the dawn of the French New Wave, and John Huston's brilliant and moving critique of an American boxer in the twilight of his career, *Fat City*. That I have neglected such classics for so long is shameful for someone who professes to be a lover of the cinema. Still, better late than never.

As far as television is concerned, HBO's *Boardwalk Empire* has proved easily the most satisfying series I have discovered this year, thanks to a tip from my professor, Richard Gwyn. But other than Old Faithful *Frasier*, I think the only other programme that passed the 'twenty-minute distraction' test this year was *Game of Thrones*. If you failed to be distracted from

43 Now wholly owned by my wife Liz

your problems by the sight of Daenerys Stormborn's dragon, turned to the dark side by the Night King, leader of the Whitewalkers, then destroying the Wall with his fountains of blue fire, I can only assume you are facing the death penalty.

I have read many fine books this year too, but with the perspective of time the one that lingers most vividly in the memory is *The Rings of Saturn,* by W.G. Sebald. In it, a German academic who has made his life in Britain undertakes a series of hikes around East Anglia, allowing his mind to wander as he does so. Among the many diverse subjects that occupy his thoughts as he walks are the seventeenth century polymath Sir Thomas Browne, the herring industry, the carpet bombing of Germany in World War II, and the history of silk manufacturing. My wife also read it, and it so affected both of us that earlier this year, just days before I was formally charged by the police, we made our way to the East Coast, where we walked in the footsteps of the Great One, re-tracing a few of his journeys.

One morning after breakfast we struck south from the town of Aldeburgh, past the Martello Tower, heading for the Orford Ness lighthouse, just visible on the far, flat horizon. Above us an enormous sky, filled with towering cumulus clouds, interspersed with patches of watery blue. On our left, the North Sea and, presumably, the herring; on our right, the remains of a once top-secret weapons research establishment where, amongst other things, radar was developed, and later, atomic bomb detonators were tested. A quite reasonable path soon degenerated into no more than an endless expanse of large round pebbles. Perhaps we should have paid more attention to signs which read:

NATURE RESERVE
NOT OPEN TO THE PUBLIC

Other than seabirds, we saw no sign of life at all, until a brown hare, big as a young fox, appeared from nowhere and sat in our path. We regarded each other for a long moment until he darted away towards the once forbidden zone.

After walking for nearly two hours we seemed to be no nearer the lighthouse than we were when we set out. Liz stopped in her tracks and said, "I'm sorry Steve. I can't do this any more."

I confessed I'd been feeling the same way for at least the last half-hour.

We retraced our steps, and when we finally got back to our hotel around three pm, feet and ankles feeling battered and bruised, we were so exhausted we fell on the bed and slept for nearly three hours. But even if on our journeys my mental meanderings were scarcely as varied and erudite as Sebald's, our little project did prove a minor success in keeping us from dwelling too much on what lay ahead.

Another useful diversion, no doubt inspired by Liz's trip to Japan in the summer, has been our re-discovery of Sumo wrestling. Channel 4 used to show Sumo back in the early 1990s, and when it stopped we were bereft. Then we found that the Japanese news channel NHK broadcasts the six 'Emperor's Cup' tournaments which are held each year, where all the leading professionals, or *Rikishi*, take part over fifteen days. Most eminent among them is 'Hakuho', a native Mongolian who has achieved legendary status in his adopted country. He has become, one might say, the Roger Federer of his chosen discipline, having won more Emperor's Cups, and more individual bouts, than any other wrestler in Sumo's venerable history, which goes back at least as far as medieval jousting. Despite his weight of one hundred and fifty-seven kilograms he moves with the grace and agility of a ballet dancer, effortlessly dispatching opponents who may weigh as much as sixty kilograms more than him. And the look in his eye as he sizes up an opponent is spine chilling.

The rules of Sumo are very simple. Wrestling in a *dojo*, or ring, thirteen feet in diameter, participants may only touch the floor with the soles of their feet, and may not step outside the *dojo* at all. They are not allowed to kick or punch, though slaps with the open hand are permitted, sometimes delivered with tremendous force. Bouts are often over within seconds, requiring slow-motion replays for us neophytes to work out exactly what happened. The audience, which includes very few foreigners, is highly knowledgeable. A particularly satisfying bout sees them hurling their seat cushions into the air in appreciation. Competition is over for this year, but we are both looking forward eagerly to the next tournament, which is due to begin in mid-January of next year. A lot more eagerly, I might say, than Christmas, which will be a trial as usual. But at least that will be over quickly, which is more than I can say for the *actual* trial.

*

Wednesday the third of January 2018, ten am. The final round of disclosures has been sent to my solicitor, who has forwarded them to me. This is a much shorter file, but what it contains is sensational. Here at last are the missing text messages exchanged between Florence and her psychotherapist. It is to her credit that she has held onto them for so many years; their content rather less so. In them, some of the details of their strange relationship are revealed. I should point out here I am no therapist. As I have often told patients in the past: "I don't do psychotherapy. I give medical advice". But I am still allowed to apply my common sense and experience to analyse the dialogue between Florence and her therapist, and to me at least they frequently demonstrate a bizarre mix of pycho-babble and baby-talk. Here I am referring in particular to the 'regression therapy' she deployed, guiding Florence to adopt a child-persona.

Chapter Nineteen

Most of what matters in your life takes place in your absence
– Salman Rushdie, Midnight's Children

Monday the eighth of January 2018, ten am. The sky is a uniform dirty grey, and there is a bitterly cold breeze. One of those 'two degrees, feels like minus five' days.

Three weeks to go. T minus 504 hours. I have done the washing-up, remembering that, no matter how deep the crisis one is facing, there is always the washing-up to be done. I have made my second cup of coffee of the day; my cigarettes are by my hand, as is my second whisky of the day. In my experience I have found there is no catastrophe so terrible that a coffee, a fag and a hit of whisky cannot ameliorate, at least to some extent.

I am ready to write.

There is a distinctly different quality about my mood today. Any attempt at compartmentalisation is redundant. I can't do it anymore. Precisely five hundred and four hours from now I will be standing in Courtroom Number Three with my co-accused, listening to the lawyers go through their preliminary arguments before Judge Tom Crowther, QC. Between now and then I shall have:

- drunk over a hundred units of alcohol, mostly in the form of Lidl's finest *Ben Bracken* twelve-year-old single malt whisky, though a certain quantity of dessert wine and brandy and dry ginger (my father's favourite drink) will also have been consumed. A writer using alcohol to assist the creative process? Who ever heard of such a thing?
- smoked between four and five hundred cigarettes (Benson and Hedges *Gold*, my favoured brand since my teens, though in those days they were known as "Special Filter").
- drunk over one hundred and twenty cups of coffee, usually *Cafe Direct 'Machu Picchu'* blend, instant variety.

- moved my bowels between twenty and thirty times, and micturated maybe a hundred times, perhaps twenty or so in the small hours of the night.
- masturbated once or twice, perhaps not; extreme stress, as I have found in the past, can cause sexual interest to fade away almost to nothing.
- made love. Are you kidding?
- watched about one hundred and seventy hours of television, while paying attention to hardly any of it.
- consumed innumerable 'treats': jelly babies, liquorice all-sorts, chocolate bars, and an impressive array of cheeses from Britain and around the world. But I must be careful not to put on too much weight. My suit only barely fits now, and I don't want to sit through the four weeks of the trial feeling like a trussed chicken.

I hate it when people say: "I've got some good news and some bad news. Which do you want first?" I always ask for the bad news first. Better to have the down, followed by the up, rather than the other way round.

The Bad News. My solicitor phoned me last Friday to inform me that my junior barrister has been stricken with a severe spinal disorder, and surgery is required urgently. Consequently, she has had to withdraw from the case. Fortunately my lead counsel, "CC QC" as Mark Crowley calls him, is still on board, though now he will have to conduct the case by himself. Ms Ferrier has already made some valuable contributions to my defence, most notably helping to compile the all-important 'timeline' of events, along with a number of other vital preparatory tasks. But it *is* a setback. Thank goodness Chris Clee is still on board. Without him we would have had to engage another counsel at short notice which would have been a disastrous setback at the worst possible moment.

Then there are the 'Abuse of Process' arguments. I have now read the submissions from Michael E's team, and the one from my own, both of which were presented to the court last week. To me they represent a stunning indictment on the process which has led to the accused standing in the dock, redolent as it is of mismanagement, incompetence and, dare I say it, even negligence on the part of the investigating police officers and the CPS, who have all but allowed Florence to control the investigation from its outset. Significant questions have been raised concerning the reliability of the photo-lineup, whereby Florence was able to identify Michael E as one of her abusers even though he is adamant he never once met her.

His barrister's report, which runs to twelve pages, concludes with the words:

"...Accordingly, it is submitted that it is impossible to give the defendant a fair trial and his right under Article 6 of the ECHR[44] has been denied to him.

Further or in the alternative, the failures on behalf of the prosecution and the [police] officer's actions are such that to continue proceedings would offend the Court's sense of justice and propriety and would undermine Public Confidence in the Criminal Justice system and bring it into disrepute. A stay in this case is necessary to protect the Criminal Justice system..."

Chris Clee's submission, of a similar length, proceeds along broadly similar lines, though for tactical reasons different aspects are stressed in his report. He has looked carefully at the counselling notes provided by Florence's psychotherapist, arguing that the relationship between client and therapist exceeded normal professional boundaries on numerous occasions, calling her conclusions into question:

"...On several occasions, listed in the report, the therapist uses 'transitional objects', such as teddy-bears, and also 'regression work', where it appears Florence D was encouraged to act as a child. It appears that certain disclosures may have originated from the therapist..."

He goes on to challenge the way the sixteen interviews with Florence were conducted by the police:

"...There appears to have been no interview planning and the interviews are littered with frequent inappropriate observations by the officer, such as:

'This must be massively traumatic for you'
'I can't begin to understand how you feel'
'You are very thoughtful, you really are'
'I'm here to listen... and take that burden from you'

44 European Court of Human Rights.

He closes with the following (edited) observations:

"...Florence has found a powerful ally in the police, who have acted on her allegations without question; ignoring obvious lines of enquiry and seeking to undermine potential evidence which contradicts her allegations... The Court is invited to stay the proceedings insofar as to allow the case to proceed would convey the impression the Court will adopt the approach that the end will justify the means; an approach adopted by the police throughout the course of this case..."

Pretty devastating, I think you'll agree. And just moments ago, my legal team have emailed to me the Abuse of Process arguments from all the other teams, each taking their own individual slants, but each focussing on police and CPS misconduct throughout. Aye, but here's the rub. My solicitor warns me it probably won't work. Abuse of Process arguments are often deployed, especially in complex cases, but they very rarely succeed. To stop a trial is a profound step for any judge to take, impugning the safety of the entire judicial system. So in nearly every case, the trial is allowed to proceed. We may have more luck with our 'Bad Character' application, he tells me, guaranteeing an extremely uncomfortable time on the stand for Florence. But the trial *will* go ahead.

The Good News. Just after Christmas I attended a neighbour's party where I contracted the cold he was generously distributing among his guests. In my case, as usual, it turned almost immediately to a chest infection. You always know: there is a sort of clamping-down sensation deep in the lungs; a feeling you aren't getting enough air and may shortly pass out. You don't, but it's how you feel. It's one of the worst feelings there is. Straight away I started my 'rescue pack': a broad-spectrum antibiotic and prednisolone, a potent oral steroid. As usual, the remedy takes days to work, but within twenty-four hours my limb stiffness had almost completely disappeared.

Since around the middle of August last year my muscles started tightening up; first my knees, then my hips and then my shoulders, to the point that almost any movement was painful. Sitting down and rising from a chair, putting on or taking off a coat, climbing into and out of a car, getting into and out of bed, reaching for a coffee cup or cigarette; the tightness has been with me every waking moment, and indeed woken me from my sleep on numerous occasions. Now, miraculously, it has gone. Could it be the steroids? As a doctor, I have to concede this possibility. Systemic steroids are often used to bring about remissions in cases of severe rheumatoid arthritis, and they can be extremely effective, in the short term at least. So will it all come back as soon as I stop the steroids? My course is due to finish tomorrow, so I'll soon find out.

The Confusing News. This morning, an email from Samantha Day, one of Mark Crowley's assistant solicitors. It has emerged that on the twenty-second of November last year, just before our PTR hearing, Florence claimed to have received a package containing wire which sent her into a terrible panic. This wire, normally used in the making of jewellery, was the same kind her father used to tie her up with, and, as she says in her email to Cath Orford, *the defendants would have known that.* It is also tied into knots, *the same knots her father used to use.* A photograph of the package in question is included in the email. She says that it was sent via Amazon, but when the police check, Amazon say their package was indeed used and sent to her address, but on interrogating the bar code found that *something else was sent.* Who sent the package? Did she send it to herself? We may never know.

★

Three pm. Another email from my solicitor. In the attachment, a letter he has written to the Chief Crown Prosecutor in Wales. This is his 'hand grenade', a last ditch attempt to put the prosecution off balance and force them to accept the strong likelihood that they will be seen as fools, or worse, if they are reckless enough to go ahead with the trial. Thoughtfully argued over five pages, it is, to me at least, a devastating indictment of their behaviour throughout the eighteen months of the investigation. I summarise its content as follows:

...We write as we have serious misgivings about the way this matter has been handled and request that you as the head of CPS Wales conduct an urgent and thorough review of this extraordinary case...

He mentions the five separate Abuse of Process arguments already submitted to the Court

...which highlight that there has been serious professional miscon-duct involving the police officers investigating the case and the Complainant which potentially undermines the criminal justice system. If allowed to continue this case could result in serious miscar-riages of justice and in the event of mass acquittals the Complainant could face prosecution herself for perjury...

...If convicted our client faces a substantial custodial sentence which would probably result in him dying in prison, or in the event of mass acquittals, the Complainant would be revealed as having repeatedly perjured herself over a number of years... There can be little alternative conclusion and must bring satellite litigation...

...We believe that at the time a charging decision was made in April 2017, none of the unused material had been reviewed or disclosed and the charging lawyer, under considerable pressure in view of the repeated delay, agreed charges. Had that voluminous and damaging unused material had been available and evaluated by any reviewing lawyer we submit that no charges would have been autho-rised...

Mark Crowley then proceeds to a crushing rebuttal of Florence's claim that I performed an abortion on her, this time quoting from a gynaecological expert, who happens to be one of the most renowned specialists in Britain, Professor Linda Cardozo. Her CV runs to no less than seventy pages, listing the many research projects and distinguished academic papers she has authored and co-authored over the course of her illustrious career. Why, even the letters after her name cover an entire line. This is what entitles her to command handsome fees for compil-ing her report and appearing in court on my behalf. In essence, however, her report is no different from the one I received, free of charge, from the local gynaecology consultant I approached back in August 2016. They both say her account of events is a work of the imagination. We handed the latter over to the police as long ago as September 2016, for them to relay it to the CPS, but evidence appears to suggest *they never even looked at it*. Had they done so, they might have commissioned their own expert to look at her description of events. As it is, we have seen the prose-cution's list of witnesses, and they are not intending to put any medical experts of their own on the stand. This in itself speaks volumes.

Then, and this comes as news to me, he mentions what he describes as the 'notorious floorboard incident', when the police had the brilliant idea of performing a detailed forensic examination of the attic room in my house, in which Florence claims the abortion took place, and where, she says, much blood was spilt. A search warrant was obtained, and they were all set to raid my house on the thirteenth of November last year, armed with crowbars to pull up the floorboards. But then there was a change of heart. As emails in the Unused Materials reveal (which I failed to notice in my original perusal), a conversation took place in which, despite extraordinary advances in forensic techniques, where even drops of blood invisible to the naked eye can now be detected, the police worried that they might not find anything, thereby damaging their case against me. When these emails were discovered, my team immediately wrote to the police inviting them to search the attic room and do their worst. Although the room has been re-decorated more than once since 1995, the skirting boards (which the police wanted to tear off to see what was behind them) and floorboards are the same as they were then. They never replied to our invitation.

Winding up, Mark Crowley says:

...The CPS are in danger of prosecuting these five men in what yet again could be another high-profile miscarriage of justice here in South Wales, where the police have been less than impartial, intent on pursuing these men at all costs, without properly investigating all reasonable lines of enquiry and the CPS are likely to be implicated in their failings... Our client is personally expecting to spend in excess of £100,000 defending his case, a sum which will rise significantly if the case goes to trial, and the bill to the tax payer is likely to exceed half a million pounds; this in a case in which the Complainant's accounts are incredible, inconsistent, purely self-serving, clearly undermined by medical experts and where she has a history of making false claims. If you continue with this case, we put you on public notice that that we will be seeking costs against the CPS on the basis of their neglect in failing to carry out their duty under the Code of Public Prosecutors.

...By any objective criteria this case would never have been allowed to have been charged had the unused material been available in April 2017... This case is now fundamentally flawed for the many reasons highlighted above, making the prospects of a successful conviction for any of the defendants extremely unlikely...

Three-fifteen pm. Another email from my solicitors. Although the letter above was directed to the top of the hierarchy, Mark Crowley has already had a reply from a more junior member of the CPS staff, which he has copied to me, the response, if I may paraphrase, is as follows:

Good Morning
We thank you for your letter and note its contents.
We're going ahead anyway.
Yours etc

Mark adds a footnote:

'*...As you can see we have thrown everything at this... Sadly I now feel we must prepare ourselves for a full trial and trust she cracks in evidence or the jury see through her incredible claims...*'

Mark Crowley does not say it, but it is clear to me that whoever wrote that peremptory reply has not even read his letter properly. Fifteen minutes is barely enough time to have scrutinised its five pages carefully, let alone deliver a considered response. Yet that is only typical of their behaviour, as we have seen. But it is enough to plunge me afresh into a pit of despair. When Liz comes home she can see from my face that something is wrong and demands to see the emails. Her face goes a nasty shade of putty grey as she does so. We spend a quiet, sombre evening together, exchanging few words, engrossed in our own private thoughts. What can we say? Despite all the assurances that the jury will see sense, we both know juries get it wrong: the Birmingham Six, the Guildford Four, the Cardiff Three; all cases where innocent people spent years behind bars for crimes they did not commit. And these are just the high-profile examples. There are many, many others. Owen, who has spent a lot of time researching false accusations online, has told me that at this moment there may be as many as five hundred people, mainly men, languishing in prison, wrongly convicted of crimes of sexual assault.[45] Granted, most of these are cases where there was more than one complainant, and many come out of 'reconstructed families', with step-parents involved, either as accusers or accused. These scenarios may not apply to my case, but the fact is my future remains in jeopardy.

★

Tuesday the ninth of January 2018, two pm. Another email from my solicitors. Attached is an updated response from the CPS to Mark Crowley's 'hand grenade', and this time it comes from the addressee, the head of CPS Wales himself:

Dear Mr Crowley,

...I can assure you the Chief Crown Prosecutor and myself are aware of the situation and meetings are in place to discuss the issues you raise. The matter is receiving close and urgent attention...

A difference in tone is immediately apparent.

"At least they are considering their problems", Mark says.

★

Thursday January the eleventh 2018, nine-fifteen am. It is my birthday, the Earth occupying the same position in the solar system as it did on the night of my birth, sixty-seven orbits ago. Not that it is in the same position in space. The Sun and its children have journeyed nearly thirty billion miles from their positions on the eleventh of January 1951, as the spiral arms of the Milky Way have swirled around the galactic core. And that's not the whole story. The entire galaxy is hurtling through the cosmos at a speed of 1.3 million miles per hour, so to be more accurate, our home planet is three-quarters of a *trillion* miles from where it was on the day of my birth. Never say your life is going nowhere.

Liz and I have been called to an urgent meeting with my solicitors. Later Liz will tell me that the same thing happened as usual: as soon as the realities are spelled out, my face changes colour and I start sighing deeply. I don't notice, but she says that each time I do, the team members turn and look at me in alarm.

45 Source: F.A.C.T. (Falsely Accused Carers and Teachers).

Is it surprising? The hand grenade has been thrown, but it appears to have been a dud. Once again they explain we will have to go the distance with this; more worryingly, this time there is no confident prediction of a successful outcome.

"As I suggested earlier this week, all we can hope now is that she will crack on the stand or the jury will see through her lies. By the way, I hope you realise that the first week or two of the trial are likely to be very tough on you. All the publicity will be about her allegations, and you can expect the coverage to be extremely unpleasant."

"I see."

Even now there is no advice offered as to how best to defend myself on the stand. So just before we leave, I say:

"OK, it's my birthday today, so give me just one birthday tip: when I'm sitting in the dock and I know the jury are going to be looking at me from time to time, do I shake my head vigorously when I hear Florence telling her lies?"

"Definitely not. Just sit there, look like you're paying attention obviously, but retain your dignity at all times and make no facial expression. No smirking, no head-shaking, no shouting out and no eye-rolling. Just remember: dignity, always dignity."

"OK, good. Thank you. Not a wasted day then. I've learnt something useful today."

We trudge home in silence, heads down, contemplating doomsday scenarios. I have all but convinced myself I am going down. She *won't* crack on the stand; the jury *won't* see through her lies. My muscle tightness has never been this bad. And it's going to get worse. Within days of stopping my steroids it all came back with a vengeance. I study the puddles lying on the venerable granite paving stones; glance up from time to time at the now bare and desolate trees moving in the chill breeze. I am walking the streets of my city, a 'free' man. But for how much longer? I look at Liz. The look on her face says it all.

★

Eleventh of January. Three pm. A phone call from Owen.

"Have you heard?"

"Heard what?"

"Are you sitting down?"

I hate it when people say that. I suppose it is a form of etiquette, but do people really fear I am going to fall into a dead faint the moment I hear big news?

"What is it? What's happened?"

"You haven't talked to your solicitors today?"

"As it happens, yes. I had a meeting with them this morning. Has something happened since then?"

"The CPS have dropped all charges. We're in the clear!"

"Get out of here. That isn't funny."

"It's true Steve. Contact them yourself if you want."

"I will. I'm putting the phone down now and I'll get back to you."

But Liz is already on her mobile, and hands it over when she is connected. It is Samantha Day, Mark Crowley's assistant. If Mark is the hand grenade, she is the little fox, diminutive in stature but sharp eyed, never missing a trick, forever spotting tiny details others have overlooked.

"Hi Steve. Have you looked at your inbox lately?"

I hadn't. Unusual for someone who checks his emails about once an hour, but it is true.

"If you do you'll see a letter we've copied to you from the CPS. They have dropped all charges against all the accused. It's over."

Liz, who is listening on speaker, bursts into tears and runs from the room. I can remember only two occasions in my life when shock caused me to need to sit down in a hurry. The first was when I saw the South Tower of the World Trade Centre collapse on 9/11. The second was five years later when I discovered the dead body of my son. This makes it a third. Fortunately I am already sitting down.

"So it's true?"

"Yes, Steve, it's true. The only thing left to do is to appear at the Crown Court again on Monday, so the judge can formally enter not guilty verdicts on your behalf, and also to hear the chief Crown Prosecutor explain to the judge why the case has collapsed."

"My God, I can't believe it. I, I…"

It will not sink in. I sit on my sofa in a state of numbed shock, a thousand thoughts swirling through my head at once. So the hand grenade worked. But what part? After long seconds I retain the power of speech.

"What was the killer factor, do you know?"

"We don't know yet, and we may never find out the real reasons, but Mark thinks it is the medical evidence. As you know, it was very powerful, and the prosecution had not arranged any medical experts of their own to rebut it. But as I say, we may never know the exact reasons. We'll see you in court on Monday at ten am. I'm so happy for you Steve. Oh, by the way, you might want to issue a press release, though I wouldn't tell them too much until after the hearing on Monday."

I put the phone down, a cigarette finds its way into my hand as if by magic, and Liz, who has recovered her composure, brings me a large whisky. I stand up, legs still shaky, and we have a long, long hug.

When I have calmed down a little I phone Owen back and apologise for my earlier incredulity. He is gracious, says he understands entirely. He confesses he too found it impossible to appreciate the enormity of the news at first. We will talk at length soon, but I realise I must start informing my friends about the good news. Starting with my brother, it is a long list; a long, joyous list.

But before I can get started the phone goes again.

"Hello, is that Mr Glascoe?"

"Yes."

This is DC Neil Ives here."

"What, the same guy who arrested me at Bristol airport in 2016?"

"Yes."

"The same guy who placed me in handcuffs despite my protests that it wasn't necessary?"

"Er…"

I become quite excited at this point.

"The same guy who got in my face and said 'Admit it, you were expecting us, weren't you?"

Very quickly he comes back with:

"I never said that."

"Really?"

"Look, Mr Glascoe, please calm down and listen. We have

information that the complainant has gone missing from her home, and hasn't been seen for twenty-four hours. We think it is possible she may be coming to confront you."

The whole situation appears to be approaching the point of high farce.

"So she might be waiting outside for me with a large axe or meat cleaver?"

"No, no, we just thought you should know we have placed a marker on your house.[46] so if you see her, or see any unusual activity in your street you should ring 999 and a police car will attend your address immediately."

"Is this about the fact that I've been cleared of all charges against me?"

"What? Why do you say that?"

It now becomes apparent we have been informed before the police, which I find rather surprising. I confirm that I have seen a letter from the CPS which has been forwarded to me by my solicitor. I get the feeling he doesn't believe me; presumably he is as shocked as I was half an hour ago. I thank him for his concern and the call is ended. I look at Liz, who has again been listening on speaker.

"Well, we've known for some time that she reserved particular hatred for me over and above all the other defendants, so, do you think she's out there now, waiting for me with an axe in her hands?"

"I doubt it, but I'll have a look if you like."

She picks up a kitchen knife and wanders out into the street. In a moment she is back, shaking her head.

"Nothing?"

"Nothing."

"Do you think it's real?"

"Nah. She hasn't got the balls, despite all her talk of wanting to stab you in the heart."

We quickly put this highly improbable scenario out of our minds and settle to our glorious task of informing our friends and loved ones, but not before I send an email to the BBC news desk, explaining the situation. Finally, after nearly two hours I stop, having reached the end of the list. I feel completely

---

46 For six months, although we only found this out later.

drained. Liz has been doing the same with all her friends. We had already booked a birthday meal at a local Indian restaurant for this evening, though at this moment my appetite has vanished. Liz feels the same, but insists we go anyway. I take my four-foot ash walking staff with me, having decided it is the best defensive weapon to keep any potential axe-murderess at arm's length. Normally I only use it when walking in the country, but these are exceptional circumstances. We walk the half-mile to the restaurant, looking over our shoulders and taking more interest in passers-by than is usual, but see nothing untoward. Once sat down at our table, as often happens in such situations, we find that when food is placed in front of us, we remember how hungry we are and wolf it down with a will.

Friday the twelfth of January 2018, eleven am. A call from the BBC. I'm glad they have called. Although I can understand their reasons, I remain a little resentful that they showed my image on the television news, naming me though not the other defendants. So the first thing I say is that 'The Man in the White Hat' wants to be pictured again, in his white hat, emerging from the court a free man. They confirm this will definitely happen, and also request an interview which may be conducted at my home if I would like that. I would like that. I must check with my legal team what I am allowed to say; I don't want to be sued for slander or breach of confidentiality. But whatever has emerged into the public domain already, such as the revelations at my PTR hearing in November, and what comes out of the hearing on Monday, will be fair game. I shall want to speak about the circumstances of my arrest; the partisan approach of the police and how they had convinced themselves we were guilty from the outset; and the incompetence of the CPS in coming to a charging decision without looking at all the facts. But I think I will concentrate on the effect all this has had on us. We have been *injured* by all this, profoundly injured, though I will be careful to say it has not "ruined our lives". I hate it when people say that. Our lives have been damaged; that cannot be denied, but they have not been *ruined*.

The strange thing is that today, nearly twenty-four hours on from my reprieve, *I don't feel any different*. My muscle tightness is, if anything, worse than yesterday, and my mind remains in turmoil. I still find myself thinking, how am I going to manage on the stand, and then realise, wait, it isn't going to happen. I'm never going to appear on the stand. It's over. But the tension, the anxiety, the fear, somehow it is all still there. It is very strange. But then, I have been feeling this way for more than seventy-eight weeks; it would be naïve to expect it all to evaporate in a few hours. My guess: after the hearing on Monday, I will begin to feel different, but it will still be weeks or even months before I get back to 'normal', and return to my perennial preoccupations: missing my son Seth, idly speculating as to how long I will live, while fearing the elephant and the rhino might become extinct before I do, and, of course, wondering if I will ever get this book published. To add to those, perhaps a couple of contemporary concerns that have all but passed me by over the past year and a half: worrying about how much damage the Brexit process is going to do to Britain, and how much damage the Trump presidency is going to do to the whole world.

Sunday January the fourteenth 2018, one pm. Prior to visiting my mother, I am walking along the famous coastal path between Ogmore-by-Sea and Southerndown,[47] and at last, nearly seventy-two hours on, I *am* beginning to feel a little better. As a bright winter sun lights up the sea, and a gentle southerly breeze ruffles my hair, it occurs to me that it *does* feel different this time: different from all the times I have come out to the South Wales coast over the last eighteen months, nearly one hundred and fifty times in all. On all those occasions, and at nearly every other time, I have borne the heavy weight of false allegations; knowing it is not impossible the jury will believe them, and that I could find myself spending the remainder of my life in prison.

I have never spoken of my problems to my mother. It would be a terrible cruelty. With her severe Alzheimer's she would forget the details within a minute. However, because even in advanced memory loss the emotional sense is retained intact, she might find herself distraught without knowing why. So every

47 The celebrated Welsh poet Dannie Abse observed: "If there's a finer coastal walk than the one between Ogmore and Southerndown, it's the one between Southerndown and Ogmore."

time I visited her I pretended I was fine, and hoped her still acute emotional antennae didn't pick anything up. I don't think they did. Now, at last, I don't need to pretend anymore.

Today my step is lighter, my head is held higher and I am happy to look my fellow walkers in the eye and offer a brief greeting. This is how I always used to behave; today, it seems, I can do it once again.

Looking into the bright sky, I notice my Weiss ring again. It is a nuisance sometimes, but on the whole I am getting used to my little fly. There is no option really, as Mr Kumar warned me it would most likely be permanent. But as he predicted, there would be days when I hardly noticed it at all, and that has turned out to be true. And at least the retinal detachment I so feared never materialised.

Liz told me this morning that throughout the Christmas period she kept wondering whether it would be the last one she would ever spend with me; whether she would shortly discover what it would be like to spend night after night without me beside her, and how it would be to eat all her meals by herself. Recent events have taken a terrible toll on us, and not only us, but our friends and loved ones as well. In the last three days they have been ringing up to tell me exactly this, some breaking down on the phone as they expressed their joy at my last-minute reprieve, only now able to reveal how deeply it had affected them. Just a few days ago, for example, one of our oldest and dearest friends had invited us to her New Year's celebrations, in which we invariably take part. On this occasion, however, we felt too upset to attend. She in turn became so distraught she drank far too much far too quickly and made herself horribly ill.

Chapter Twenty

Things fall apart. The centre cannot hold.
— *W.B. Yeats*

Good morning to all! It is Monday the fifteenth of January 2018, ten am. Outside there is a persistent, drenching rain; in spite of that it is relatively mild. One might say, a pretty typical winter's day in South Wales. Liz and I have just been filmed by the BBC entering the court (they made us do it three times because their camera lens kept fogging up in the humid conditions).

Just before we enter the courtroom, I spot Chris Clee. Extremely tall, topped out with a thatch of silver hair, there is a subtle reference to his near-homonym, Christopher Lee. Seeing me, he draws me aside and says:

"I just wanted you to know that in all my time at the bar I have never encountered such a tissue of lies as those peddled by your accuser. You're going to hear the prosecution barrister speak of a 'medical procedure' in a moment. I know because I've already seen the transcript. But blink and you'll miss it."

But he is gone, trailing a subliminal wreath of mist behind him before I have a chance to ask him what he means.

Outside the courtroom there is a joyous, almost crystalline feeling in the air. Although everyone is speaking in hushed tones, the atmosphere is strangely reminiscent of a childhood Christmas. Having made certain not to be late, all my fellow accused are there already: Owen, wearing the biggest grin of his life, sits with his wife, who is still looking shell-shocked. There is Eric E, with his wife, chatting quietly to their barrister, while in the corner is Michael E, talking in whispers with his partner. Finally, Simon C, his wife by his side, is also conferring with his lawyer. They all look literally years younger than when I last saw them. I make the announcement that I am writing a memoir and tell them the alternate names I have given them. They all approve of my choices, and express relief I will be preserving their anonymity.

Inside the courtroom, Catherine Richards, Chief Crown Prosecutor, takes to her feet and mutters something about offering no evidence and there being "no longer any realistic prospect of conviction". I try to take notes but it is hard to hear what is being said. I think I hear something about "medical evidence casting doubt on the complainant's reliability", but I'm not sure. If she offered any explanation for this "medical evidence" I didn't hear it, but it must have been important for it to have mentioned at all. But I definitely heard something about the infamous 'package of wire' incident.

She sits down and now we are listening to Judge Tom Crowther officially entering not guilty verdicts on behalf of all the defendants. First we are asked, in turn (me first), if we are present, and then, performed so perfunctorily you would have missed it had you so much as sneezed, the deed is done. It is almost as if he had said:

"You lot in the dock: you're all not guilty of everything. You are excused. You may leave the Court. Well, go on then, what are you waiting for?"

All the others leave the court, but I stay on in the public gallery, because I want to hear Chris Clee argue for my costs. Even though I am self-funding, I am automatically entitled to have some of my solicitor's and barristers' costs refunded, though unfortunately not my expert witness fees. And not, more significantly, my Silk's fee, which forms the majority of my expenses. His arguments don't amount to much, as he warned me before proceedings began. But there will be another day in court, perhaps months away, when the arguments will be thrashed out in more detail, and flesh put on the bones of the 'skeleton argument' we made against the actions of the CPS. Only then will a decision be made, though, as he warns me, it may not go in my favour. My presence will not be required but, as I tell him, try and keep me away. Today only the briefest summary of the prosecution's reasons for abandoning the case has been offered, but there is more to come. Today, as Mark Crowley suggested, it might have been the medical evidence from my two experts that was cited as being "particularly damaging to the prosecution's case", though precisely *which* medical evidence wasn't made clear.

As mentioned above, there is also a mumbling reference to the 'package of wire', which in Catherine Richards's words "might cast doubt on the complainant's credibility". Might? One possible explanation, of course, is that Florence sent the package to herself, though she has never admitted that. The judge concludes by saying there may a need for "internal proceedings" against individual police officers and members of the CPS staff, while adding this is not in his domain, "but for others to determine". Will anyone face disciplinary action over this fiasco, or even lose their jobs? We may never find out. Then the judge rises and we all file out.

As we are leaving the thought occurs to me that there are no atheists in foxholes, or in the dock for that matter. So, thank you God. And thank you Mark Crowley. As my personal saviour, you're just one step down from Him in my book.

Outside the courtroom I am approached by Simon, who asks me not to release his name in any interviews I might give. I tell him not to worry. He adds that on the day he was arrested, he informed the police of critical exculpatory evidence on his computer and invited them to inspect it there and then. No need to send the computer to any high-tech crime lab. And what did the police do? Nothing. They just took hold of his computer, snapped the lid shut and tucked it away in a storeroom for month after month, gathering dust, untouched by any human hand.

Monday fifteenth of January. Two pm. The media arrive in force. First I am interviewed for BBC Radio Wales and Radio 5 Live. Then it is BBC TV's turn. I thought they were going to conduct their interview in our kitchen, as the radio reporter did, but no, there's the 'wrong kind of light' in there, so we repair to our front room and, to my surprise, the curtains are drawn and a photo-flood used instead. In what seems like semi-darkness I go through the issues one by one. It isn't hard: I've been rehearsing this interview in my mind for months. Later it is shown on the six-thirty and ten-thirty bulletins. For a few brief hours my story occupies a prominent position in the newsfeeds of virtually all media outlets. Every few minutes my phone goes off, as congratulatory text messages and emails start rolling in. When I watch the footage I am shocked by how old and jowly I look, though I am glad that in the two minutes I was allotted I was able to make at least some of the points I wanted to bring out.

Later the police issue a press statement in which they defend their actions vigorously. They say they are "disappointed" by the collapse of the case, which to me clearly implies they still believe we are all guilty, regardless of what the judge said. To them it's as if we had 'got off on a technicality'.

Yes, they communicated with her electronically, but as she lived outside the Cardiff area this was necessary in order to keep her updated and support their 'vulnerable complainant'. But this misses the point entirely. It is not the *fact* of the communications; it is the *nature* of them that is of concern.

I send their statement to Owen, who is furious, resolved to get payback for their mishandling of the case. I wish him the best of luck but warn him it won't be easy. Professional guilds such as the police protect their own with furious tenacity, and in my view an official complaint won't get very far. But I applaud the fact that he's going to try. I tell him I'm going to write to my MP,[48] and invite him to do the same.

I needed this. I needed the BBC to show me emerging from the court cleared of all charges to balance the coverage of me leaving the court in November of last year, having been accused of hideous sexual crimes against a young girl. I needed to put the record straight for the benefit of all the people who had only heard I was in some kind of trouble over offences against 'girls', as they put it.

★

Who is to blame for all this? How come five innocent men only narrowly avoided falling victim to a terrible miscarriage of justice? To me, there are four distinct components:
1. Florence: a woman who, it seems, was perfectly happy to see

---

48 I did contact Jo Stevens, and was granted a face-to-face interview. She was horrified to learn the details of the case. Interestingly, she knew little about the inner workings of CICA, but promised to find out more.

five men rot in prison, all for a little bit of money. Obviously this would not be her view. I am confident that if interviewed today she would insist that there has indeed been a gross miscarriage of justice, and that five evil men have walked free due to a catastrophic dereliction of duty by the police and the CPS. And furthermore, I think I am safe in saying, she would maintain the complaints she made against us were *not* motivated by money. Far from it. She was only claiming that to which she was entitled under the law.

Owen had told me he believes *I* may be to blame for him being charged. My failure to inform the police that I was mistaken when I said he might have been present at some of those parties could have made the difference in the decision to charge him. But he is wrong. I said he *might* have attended one or two parties, but that *I wasn't sure*, it was so long ago. But Florence *was* sure. She was one hundred per cent certain he *had* been there and it was where he had participated in her abuse. That's why he was charged. Just to be clear, I believe him when he says he didn't attend any of the parties in question.

2. Cath Orford and friends at South Wales Police. These people not only believed every word Florence told them, they continued to pursue us in the face of evidence that contradicted Florence's version of events.[49] Doubtless they felt they were doing their jobs as well as they could. Doubtless they did not intend to cause harm. No doubt, too, their desire to obtain justice – or what they believed justice to be – was their overriding motivation. But it is hard to avoid the conclusion that they ignored one of the fundamental precepts of police work: that *all* lines of enquiry should be pursued, whether they lead towards, or away from, the accused. And this despite the damning findings of Sir Richard Henriques's 2016 report on the Metropolitan Police's handling of *Operation Midland*, which highlighted this as being one of the fundamental problems underlying that investigation. You may recall how serial fantasist 'Nick'[50] was believed when he claimed half of Westminster was

---

49 This is a classic example of what is known as 'confirmation bias', a scourge of clear thinking in many professions, including medicine.

involved in a paedophile ring, resulting in the very public excoriation of several public figures, including Leon Brittan, Lord Bramhall and Harvey Proctor.

3. The Crown Prosecution Service. Overworked, underpaid, under pressure from above, they accepted the police's conclusions unquestioningly, failing to review vital information that could have exonerated us months ago. We learned later that no less than four prosecutors had been assigned to the case, in part due to one of them taking a lengthy leave of absence on health grounds. But this inevitably led to continuity issues, which my defence team believe led them to adopt the 'safe' position of "if in doubt, prosecute".

4. Alison Saunders, Director of Public Prosecutions. She is the one who, some years ago now, invited the public to bring forward their claims of rape and historical sexual abuse, promising them in as many words: "You will be *believed.*" And the call, as we have seen, has been taken up by police forces around the country.[51] I submit what she should have said was: "You will be taken *seriously,* and your claims will be investigated thoroughly and *objectively.*" I realise her view reflects the need for change in the attitudes of the police, who in the past have failed to support victims of sexual abuse properly. But the balance should not swing too far in the other direction. Immediately assuming an accused person is guilty is no better than disbelieving a complainant.

It gets worse. In October of last year she was interviewed by John Humphrys on the Today programme, and stated:

"Just because an accused is found not guilty in court, doesn't mean the allegations were false."

Really, Alison? So on that basis, maybe you think *I'm* guilty too? Even though my accuser has been exposed as a serial fantasist, motivated by financial gain? I know she was referring to the high standard of proof necessary in courts, but when I was

---

50 In July 2018 the CPS announced plans to prosecute 'Nick' (Carl Beech) for perverting the course of justice. They're also doing him for fraud, in connection with the £22,000 he claimed from CICA.

51 In March 2018, Alison Saunders announced she would be leaving her post as head of the CPS in October. That very day, Metropolitan Police Commissioner Cressida Dick said the Met was dropping its policy of automatically believing all complainants of historical sexual abuse.

growing up, I developed the naïve belief that if someone was found guilty in a court of law, they *did it*, or at least probably did. Conversely, if they were found not guilty, they probably *didn't*. According to Alison Saunders, that isn't right anymore, if indeed it ever was.

Well, here's something else that isn't right: I suggest the current system where complainants are financially compensated before any corroborating evidence emerges is wrong. In Germany victims of sexual abuse are not rewarded financially, but are offered emotional support and psychotherapy, funded by the state. That, presumably, is what they need. Giving out large sums of cash carries a significant risk of encouraging false accusers.

Finally, the anonymity rule. Rules regarding the anonymity of suspects were changed by Act of Parliament in 1992. But with increasing numbers of cases like mine, Parliament may need to revisit it. I am aware of the counter-argument; that publicising the names of suspects gives the opportunity for other victims to come forward, but what often happens in practice is that other false accusers come out of the woodwork, anxious to make an easy buck. We saw this in the case of Cliff Richard, who was never even arrested. After the tsunami of publicity about him broke, several other bogus victims came forward. Thank goodness common sense prevailed, and Cliff's name was cleared. Others are not so fortunate.

I realise I am on dangerous ground here. I am only too aware that my call for a more objective attitude among the investigating authorities will not go down well in some quarters. I get the distinct impression that challenging the current *status quo* is in some way politically incorrect. This explains why left-of-centre newspapers such *The Guardian* and *The Independent* have given very little coverage to cases such as ours. I can understand the position of some left-leaning members of the establishment who seek to put an end to the old patriarchy, and in many ways I agree with them. All I would say to them is this: wait till it happens to you; wait till you or one of your loved ones is falsely accused: then you might see things a little differently.

Back last summer Liz and I attended a performance of Arthur Miller's *The Crucible* at Cardiff's New Theatre. It was an appalling production, with so many of the main players unavailable (was there some sort of actor's strike?) that most of their understudies were reduced to reading from scripts. Even so, Miller's portrayal of innocent parties being persecuted because of accusations by hysterical girls struck home. When he wrote his play in the nineteen-fifties, he was seeking to draw an analogy between those terrible events in Salem and the McCarthy witch hunts. But I couldn't stop thinking about my own predicament; that I and my fellow-accused were facing a kind of witch hunt of our own. And while those girls in the play may not have been totally blameless, at least they weren't motivated by the prospect of a cash payout.

It occurs to me now I don't hate Florence any more. In any event hate is not a feeling that sits easily with me. Until recently. But now my hate has gone, I find myself feeling sorry for her. Everything I have learned about Florence, and I feel I know her better now than most of my friends, suggests she is a deeply unhappy person, and I worry about the effect of all this on her mental wellbeing going forward. I know she has tried and failed to destroy me, but I hope she can put this behind her and move on with her life, and not try to destroy anyone else.

Tuesday the sixteenth of January, one pm. My doctor phones with good news. I had been getting steadily more paranoid about my joint stiffness, especially since it was eased by the steroids and then returned with a vengeance when they were stopped. I started to fantasise I had developed a condition known as polymyositis, a rare condition taken as sign of grave omen because it is often a sign of underlying malignancy. Polymyositis is *relieved by steroids* in its early stages. Worse, its symptomatology is identical to the symptoms I had developed in the previous months. As I have smoked all my adult life I convinced myself I was nursing early lung cancer. I was giving myself a few months to live at best. Shame, I thought, just when I had just won through one terrible ordeal only to be taken down by another.

Doctors make the worst patients, it is said, and though my GP (who reminded me of that) was sceptical of my fears we both knew he would not be able to allay my fears completely until he had performed a battery of blood tests and a chest radiograph. All had come back normal, he reported, leaving the doom-laden scenario I had painted for myself in tatters. My time has not come yet, it would seem.

Chapter Twenty-One

I fought the law and – the law won
– Bobby Fuller

Wednesday the seventeenth of January 2018, eleven am. I am phoned by David Brown from *The Times* and give him his interview. We go through the main 'bullet-points' of the story, all the way from my arrest at Bristol airport to our exoneration in court just forty-eight hours ago. When we get to the child torture allegations, he says:

So 'Florence'; that's what you're calling her in your memoir, is that right?"

"That's it."

"So you're saying she knew your son was dead when she made these accusations?"

"That's correct."

There is a long moment of silence. I hear him take a deep breath. Then he says:

"She knew."

"Yes."

Saturday the twentieth of January 2018, eight am. It has been a very strange few days. Today should have been T(rial) day minus nine; in the event it is F(reedom) day *plus* nine. I find myself feeling ten times happier, but no less stressed. The reality is that I and all my fellow accused are now probably developing a form of post-traumatic stress disorder.

All week friends and loved ones have been ringing up, falling into two groups: those who knew what has been happening and wanting to tell me "We never doubted you for a moment!", and those who who only learnt of the case through the media, saying "Oh Steve! You poor thing! It must have been terrible for you!"

Yesterday a full page of *The Times* was devoted to the case, under the headline:

Paedophile trial collapses over lurid claims of 'serial fantasist'

It featured a small photograph of me looking pensive in my garden, while most of the facing page was occupied by the case of Oliver Mears, a nineteen-year-old university student whose trial for rape also collapsed just days before his trial was due to begin.[52] My leading counsel, Chris Clee, is quoted at length in the article on my case:

"...The complainant had throughout manipulated the proceedings, disclosing alleged incidents of abuse as and when it suited her purposes; these allegations emerging through counselling sessions which of themselves are of dubious standing... She [Florence] has found a powerful ally in the police, who have shown astonishing naïveté in believing her every word, ignoring obvious lines of enquiry and, worst of all, seeking to undermine potential evidence that contradicts her allegations..."

The article also quoted the judge as saying there ought to be internal proceedings as a result of the collapse of the case, while adding that key phrase: "Obviously this is not in my domain." Just whose domain it is remains unclear to me.

The article also mentioned the letter from my gynaecologist colleague, who speculated that Florence might have based her account of the alleged abortion on sequences shown on the BBC television programme *Call the Midwife*. This was taken up by the *Mail Online* website, which ran a large still from that programme above its coverage of the proceedings. For a few brief hours, it seems, I am big news.

In the afternoon, my route guided by *Google Maps*, I made my way on foot to the Drivers Training Centre, to be lectured on the dangers of speeding and thereby avoid my points. But it led me to entirely the wrong location, and I found myself wandering hopelessly around an urban landscape which was completely alien to me. I phoned my wife in desperation, saying "I'm lost! I have no idea where I am!"

---

52 We are not alone. Last year, 916 cases were dropped at the last moment due to 'failure to disclose' issues. (source: CPS; BBC freedom of information request)

I had allowed what I thought was easily enough time to make the journey, but now the deadline was fast approaching and I was nowhere near where I needed to be. Liz jumped in her car and came down to find me. At last, many minutes later, she pulled up beside me and we sped, ironically, to the correct location.

"It wasn't easy to find you", she said. "I should have had you micro-chipped."

By the time we arrived I had missed the deadline and now I must re-book, incurring a further £45 booking fee.

Last night I received a call from Simon, who said he had read the piece in *The Times*, and praised the tone of the article. He wasn't so sure about the photograph they printed of Owen, however, which showed him wearing a broad grin.

"There's nothing to smile about in any of this," he said.

I am up writing early this morning because once again I have taken my wife to the station for an early train to London. She has to attend yet another meeting of one the several professional bodies to which she is affiliated. Driving home I tuned into the *Today* programme to hear a quote from Lord Judge, one of the country's leading jurists. Referring to the collapse of two high-profile rape cases this week, he said he feared rapists might now walk free, as juries lose confidence in the CPS's ability to prepare their cases properly. But if that is true, and I fear it may well be, then it isn't hard to work out at whose door the responsibility should be laid.

Wednesday the twenty-fourth of January 2018, eleven-thirty am. Running a few errands in the city, I found myself close to my old surgery, and for the first time in over eighteen months I decided to show my face. As soon as the staff saw me it was all hugs and kisses, the receptionists fussing round me like so many mother hens. It seems they'd all seen the television coverage.

"Oh, doctor, you poor thing! It must have been so terrible for you!" they said. Debbie, the practice manager, said, "Well I must say, doctor, after everything you've been through, you're looking remarkably well."

I only stayed a few minutes, but those minutes were among the most beautiful I have ever known.

Later that day a friend dropped round a cutting from *The Times,*
featuring an OpEd by the distinguished commentator Daniel
Finkelstein. Under the headline

Prosecutors don't know how biased they are

he quoted the head of the CPS, Alison Saunders, describing the
recent failures to secure convictions in high profile rape cases as
"disappointing and irritating", and stressed the need to get the
job done properly. She added that she is confident that no
innocent person has been jailed as the result of such an error.
That response, according to Danny Finkelstein, isn't good
enough. He went on to say this:

*"...Our 'confirmation bias' – an elementary part of social
psychology – explains how we seek comfort in every piece of evidence
that confirms we are right and find a way of excluding anything that
suggests we are wrong. Or even turning it around in our heads so that
it becomes supportive. How does someone get it wrong after exchanging 1000 texts with an unreliable complainant? Precisely because
they've exchanged 1000 texts with her..."*

Thursday the twenty-fifth of January 2018, eleven am. I get a
phone call from David Brown, *The Times* reporter who wrote
our story:

"I thought you might be interested to know Florence has
decided to make a complaint against us for our coverage of the
story."

Apparently she had engaged a firm of solicitors to write on
her behalf, saying that there was a significant error in the copy,
namely that they had stated Florence had admitted sending the
package of wire to herself, whereas that was incorrect; she had
made no such admission at any time. An apology and retraction
were therefore demanded.

"What are they going to do?"

"Well, I can't see them apologising or printing any kind of
retraction. They may be prepared to admit privately that a small
mistake had been made, but then we could also argue that if she
didn't send it, who did? After all, the packaging had come from
Amazon to her, but containing something else. And anyway,
there was no way she could be identified through the article, so

who has been defamed?"

He concluded by saying *The Times's* lawyers would probably respond in that vein and see what happened.[53]

"We found it a bit odd that Florence had gone through a firm of solicitors to make her complaint. After all, any member of the public may complain to a newspaper, free of charge."

*

Sunday the eleventh of February 2018, eight-thirty pm. I am in the BBC studios in the Llandaff district of Cardiff, left alone in a tiny soundproof booth, awaiting my interview with Stephen Nolan of BBC Radio 5 Live. It seems like an age waiting for a voice to come out of my headphones, but right on time he comes on the line and the interview begins. Nolan gives me every opportunity to go through the details of the case, and to catalogue the emotional toll it has exacted upon both of us. At one point, however, I am put severely off balance when I talk about Alison Saunders' policy of believing all complainants of historical sexual abuse.

"We've spoken to a spokesperson from the CPS, and they deny she ever said that."

I should have responded that this was disingenuous at best. By now everyone knows the culture of believing complainants started at the top and trickled down to CPS teams and police forces across the country. *L'esprit de l'esacalier* is all well and good, but in the event I was so stunned by this baldfaced denial that all I could come up with was an incredulous "Really?"

But it was only a small glitch in an otherwise favourable exchange. Over the course of a full thirty minutes, Nolan deployed all his characteristic sensitivity and grace to help me navigate my way through the details of my long, arduous journey.

*

---

53 We heard later nothing happened for quite a while. Eventually *The Times* contacted Florence's lawyers to ask what was going on. They told them they had received "no instructions" from their client.

Last night I dreamed I was dreaming. I knew I was dreaming because when I looked down at my hands I was wearing two gold rings. That cannot be right because I wear only a single platinum wedding band. I was standing atop a tall building and, knowing I was dreaming, I knew it would be safe to jump. I launched myself into space and fell, or rather dived towards the ground, my arms stretched out in the classic swallow pose. But just as a falcon in a stoop dramatically levels out within feet of the ground, I too avoided the pavement and soared into the sky. Soon I was among the clouds, feeling an almost indescribable sense of bliss. But suddenly my joy was replaced by a sense of nameless horror. Out of nowhere something seemed to overtake me from behind, a small dark object, which attached itself to my right forearm. Its outline was indistinct; I could not see it clearly. I attempted to pull it away with my left hand, but as I did so, there was a sharp pain, as though it had locked on to my skin with a series of barbs or claws. I reached into a pocket and found a long, slim pen, and with my left hand, my writing hand, I plunged the pen deep into the body of the dark object, which shuddered and fell away. I woke up.

★

Friday the twenty-seventh of April 2018, two pm. Nearly three months on from the day of our exoneration, nearly three months since, with less than two weeks to go before my trial and the verdict hanging in the balance, I was facing some of the darkest moments of my life. I had been noticing my lawyers becoming gradually less bullish about the outcome for some time. Back in the summer of 2016 Mark Crowley had told me I stood a better than ninety per cent chance of being acquitted, but as the months wore on I could detect his enthusiasm beginning to wane. Then came the terrible moment the following summer when Owen told me of some research he had uncovered during his work with other falsely accused people. He found that juries are less likely to believe a defendant in cases of historical sexual abuse than they are in cases of contemporary rape, and that the acquittal rate in the former may be as low as fifty per cent. Thus in January 2018, when we heard from the CPS that they saw no reason not to go ahead despite the 'hand-grenade letter', I realised the full extent of the danger I was facing.

Of course as we have seen, events took a very different turn and I am now a free man, my name cleared. Do I feel better now the threat of life imprisonment has been lifted? Annoyingly, the answer is yes and no. Obviously my morale has been transformed, but just as I feared, my body continues to lag behind in its apprehension of reality. My muscles, especially those of my shoulder girdle, remain tight, resulting in little stabs of pain every time I move. As February passed into March and my physical problems showed no sign of lessening, I became a very bitter, angry and resentful man. In the small hours of the night, when the little tweaks of pain would often wake me; in the mornings when the pains were at their worst; at any time when I struggled to put a coat on or remove it, I would rail against a woman who was happy to see me and four other men rot in prison. And against the injustices of a system which very nearly allowed her to do so. Sometimes I would literally roar with rage, bruising my throat in the process.

"This is all down to her, that monster! She did this to me! I'd like to fucking KILL her!"

It was eventually Liz who pointed out my folly:

"Look Steve, you really aren't helping yourself with all this anger. I think you might actually be slowing your recovery by going on like this. I don't know how, but somehow you've got to get past it."

I decided to seek solace in music. The ambient music of Brian Eno and The Orb, and especially the minimalist work of Steve Reich seemed to be what I needed to hear. Finally, when I played his marvellous *Music for 18 Musicians* the tears flooded out of me. Looking back, I think this was the moment that marked the beginning of my emotional recovery. After this I noticed my levels of drinking and smoking were beginning to fall, and without any real effort on my part: a sure sign of improvement.

Friday the twenty-seventh of April, two thirty pm. Liz and I are once again in Courtroom Number Three at Cardiff Crown Court to hear my leading counsel Christopher Clee, 'CC QC', argue the case before Judge Tom Crowther for my costs to be reimbursed by the CPS. Just before we entered the court Mark showed me the final bill: £101,000.

I am not in the dock this time, nor even in the public gallery. We have been conducted to the body of the court, and are sitting in the comfortable, padded seats usually reserved for solicitors. Here at least we can hear every word that is said. Also present in the press box is *Times* journalist David Brown, who wrote the first story about our case in January. There is no one in the public gallery.

I was at my dentist's the other day when another man sat down in the waiting room. He was wearing a smart suit in dark blue, black patent-leather shoes and a white silk shirt. But no tie. He looked so suave, so urbane, so effortlessly sophisticated that I have decided to adopt the same dress code today. In the past I have always worn a tie in court, but today there seems scarcely any point. I feel sure my fate has been decided already, regardless of my sartorial appearance. I might just as well have turned up in yoga pants.

After a brief hearing for another case, in which, interestingly, the CPS formally drops the charges against a man who has spent the last four months on remand on charges of theft, Judge Crowther, resplendent in his livery of black, scarlet and mauve, indicates to Chris Clee that he may begin.

The judge. Kind of small, isn't he?

Yeah. But he more than makes up for that with his intensity.

My brief has to prove, to the satisfaction of the judge, that the charges brought by the CPS were the result of an 'improper act or omission'.

"Your Honour, the prosecutors should have been alerted to the poor credibility of the victim by notes from 229 counselling sessions, which included 'regression work', whatever *that* is".

The counselling notes, he continues, made it clear that the therapist "had exceeded any professional boundaries" and given the woman the idea that she had been raped by five men.[54] Prosecutors had originally demanded to see the notes before deciding whether to charge, but a senior police officer had urged them to

---

54 It isn't quite as simple as that. Florence was making claims of sexual abuse and rape long before she ever met the therapist in question. It is true, however, that her claims became a lot more lurid *after* that. And it is also true all the horrific claims of child torture *did* emerge through these sessions.

take a 'victim-centric position', so they went ahead anyway. And this 'victim-centric' approach seemed to encompass sanctioning a highly unusual and inappropriate relationship developing between the complainant and the lead investigating police officer.

"Victim-centric position"? Isn't that what this case is all about?

Precisely. It sums up pretty neatly the injustice of the whole thing, I reckon.

Powerful stuff you might think. But Catherine Richards, Chief Crown Prosecutor, takes these bouncers and bashes them all over the park. She concedes the case was dropped over "considerable concern" about the detective, and that a jury might find there had been a "mirror of undue influence" by the alleged victim on the officer and the therapist. Then of course there was the small matter of that package of wire, alleged by the complainant to have been sent to her by one of the defendants, though a police investigation subsequently showed that the parcel packaging must have originated from an item ordered by a member of her own household. This catches the attention of the judge.

"Yes, that was dynamite", he concedes.

But, Catherine Richards contends, the CPS did nothing wrong in pursuing the case. "Prosecutors must be allowed a wide degree of discretion in coming to their charging decisions", she argues, and worryingly, the judge nods in agreement. Summing up, he reminds all present that it must be proved that no *reasonable* prosecutor would have decided to bring charges based on the evidence. As I understand it, this is more or less the same way cases of medical negligence are decided. When deciding such cases, the General Medical Council has to decide whether the actions of an accused doctor are consistent with those of a 'good' doctor, acting diligently and to the highest modern standards. If they are, the doctor has no case to answer. And in this case, the judge says, malpractice by the prosecution has manifestly *not* been proved.

"In the court's view the prosecution followed a course which was *in line with enlightened modern practice*".[55]

Chris Clee tries again. What about the timing of her allegations? That despite having had abundant opportunity during

---

55 Liz told me afterwards she detected a hint of irony in these words; I have to say I didn't spot it.

nearly sixteen hours of interviews with the police, Florence somehow 'forgot' to mention I had performed an abortion on her until after I had been arrested and denied all the charges? Of no relevance, snaps the judge. You can't expect a complainant to be linear in her recollections. Move on.

Mr Clee tries one final thrust, pointing out that the prosecution had had in their possession for some time a report from a world-renowned gynaecologist, which describes Florence's account of the abortion as "wholly implausible and having no possible basis in scientific fact". Judge Crowther brushes the objection aside:

"The complainant was describing a back-street abortion. The actual details are of no relevance."

I can scarcely believe my ears. "The actual details are of no relevance"? How can that be? This case is all about detail. And scientific detail has to be the most important of all. Yet here we have just seen it cast aside as extraneous. Now we have an explanation for why the prosecution were not going to put up an expert to rebut Linda Cardozo's testimony: like the judge, in their view the actual details of Florence's 'abortion' were of no importance. I've heard fundamentalist Christians dismiss science when it interferes with their view of the world: dinosaurs were antediluvian creatures, fossils were put there by God to confuse archaeologists, carbon dating is just plain wrong, that sort of thing. But to hear a judge put forward a seemingly anti-science view is profoundly shocking to me. In the past I had always believed that the practice of law was no more or less than the application of reason, logic and common sense to any given situation. I was wrong. I am reminded of the American novelist William Gaddis's words, from his 1994 book *A Frolic of His Own*:

"...Justice? You get justice in the next world. In this world you get the law..."[56]

The judge leaves the court for a few minutes to consider his position, before returning to give his judgment. As he reads from his notes it is obvious to everyone the case has been decided in

56 I am indebted to *The Secret Barrister* for this quote, which appears in the book of the same name.

advance. He summarises his demolition of Chris Clee's arguments in a handful of carefully clipped sentences, before concluding with these words:

"I have heard nothing today to suggest there was any malpractice whatsoever on the part of the Crown Prosecution Service; therefore the plaintiff's application for remuneration through general funds is denied."

And it is over. We stand in respect as Judge Crowther stalks from the courtroom, and then we file out into the great hall to confer with my team. There I receive another blow. Mark Crowley shows me a letter from the Legal Aid Board, indicating the amount of remuneration I shall receive from them: £7,280. We knew all along Chris Clee's fee would never be refunded, but when he looks at the letter, he says "Obviously they haven't allowed my fee, but it looks like they haven't even allowed for a junior barrister's fees." He shrugs, shakes my hand energetically and is gone. I knew I would only be refunded a small fraction of my costs, but not even allowing for a barrister's fees? Despite the fact that I had been warned that something like this might happen, seeing the figures placed before me, along with Chris Clee's words is, I have to admit it, a bit of a blow. Mark assures me they will appeal the award, but again warns that such an appeal may not succeed. 94 K it is.

He also told me, almost in passing, that he had received a reply from CICA following our letter to them protesting the payment of £22,000 to Florence. His letter was accompanied by a note from me, which I characterised as a 'victim impact statement'. It was essentially a list of all the emotional and physical problems I had encountered as a result of the false allegations made against me.

Decisions to pay complainants, they said, were based on the "balance of probabilities". Apparently the term "balance of probabilities" for CICA may be translated as "If the police believe a complainant, then so do we". The decision whether to grant her a further payment was "currently under consideration". We can only hope that in the light of recent revelations, the "balance of probabilities" has shifted. But I would not be at all surprised to learn they have awarded her even more 'compensation', in view of the additional allegations she made.

The following day David Brown's piece is on page five of *The Times*, under the headline:

GP accused by 'fantasist' can't claim legal fees

Later in the day we follow as the comments on the paper's website rapidly pass the two hundred mark, almost every one supportive of my position and furious at the injustice of my case. One contributor, Nigel Evans, the conservative MP found not guilty of rape in a trial back in 2014, states he had to pay out over £130,000 to clear his name. He calls for the CPS to pay the full costs of those "dragged through the courts through no fault of their own."

Another contributor, commenting on my statement that the costs had swallowed up "most" of my life-savings, found it hard to believe a GP could only amass a hundred grand's worth of savings in the course of his life, and it is true, that figure does not represent the entirety of my liquid assets. Thank God. I still have some funds remaining, which, judging by recent events I may need should I ever be falsely accused of a serious crime in the future. But, as Liz points out, that is hardly the point. I am not a Russian oligarch or an Arab potentate; a hundred thousand pounds is not small change in my book. It is to me, and probably to you too, a life-changing amount of money. And my outlay probably helped the others too. Being handsomely rewarded for their efforts, my team did the lion's share of the work, while the other teams, funded only by the meagre returns of legal aid, doubtless did their best, but they could not afford to marshal the resources we did. There was an application by one of the defendants' lawyers to secure the services of a psychologist to examine Florence: rejected by Judge Crowther. Owen's barrister suggested a 'mistaken identity' defence at one point; Owen, bless him, refused to allow it. Additionally, the contents of Simon C's hard drive, brought to light by his barrister, containing as it did powerful exculpatory evidence would doubtless have carried great weight with the jury, even though the Prosecution did not list it among the reasons for dropping the case. Unfortunately I am unable to go into detail about this because it is not 'In the Public Domain'.

But in the last analysis I do feel my money was well spent. That, it seems, is the price of freedom in today's world. Who can put a price on freedom? I can. In today's world it would appear to be £100,000. And I would willingly have spent more to have secured that most precious of gifts.

Epilogue

A Walk By The Seaside

We are just home from a week's holiday in Sicily. It is our third excursion to that extraordinary island, and each visit reveals a new set of wonders. This time we saw the cathedral at Palermo, with its extraordinary blend of Islamic and Norman styles, wandered, shaded by an umbrella, through the 'Valley of a Thousand Temples' at Agrigento (I counted only twelve, but it was so hot I may have missed some) and bathed in the hot mud pools of Vulcano. This last was certainly a delightful experience, even if its sulphurous (though oddly, not wholly unpleasant) fumes lingered on the skin for days despite several showers. But the trip proved to be too much, too soon.

Neither of us anticipated how long it would take us to recover from the traumas of recent events. We thought the adventure would be just what we needed to "take us out of ourselves", so to speak, but in the event our ambitious itinerary, something we normally take effortlessly in our stride, almost proved too much for us. My ability to manage stress has all but collapsed since my arrest, and it was perhaps naïve to expect my coping abilities would return so quickly. Every component of our travel, planes, hire-car, shuttle buses, even as simple a thing as ordering a taxi, was accompanied by almost intolerable stress. And my muscle pains, having steadily improved in the previous month, came back with unexpected severity. Perhaps this was one occasion when we should *not* have taken a busy holiday, but opted instead for lazing on a beach. But these things are easy to see in retrospect.

My choice of holiday reading was also perhaps a little unfortunate. I opted to read *The Innocent Man* by John Grisham, a truly terrifying nonfiction account of the case of Ron Williamson, an Oklahoman railroaded by a ruthless and blinkered justice system, wrongfully convicted of first degree murder and dispatched to Death Row, all because he had a colourful personality and a somewhat chequered past. Like me, a victim of confirmation bias, Ron was at one point within three weeks of his appointment with the executioner before his case was taken up by the Innocence Project and a disastrous miscarriage of justice narrowly averted. Ron's case was even worse than my own. I at least did not face the death penalty for a crime I did not commit, but my experience did, I imagine, allow me to identify with his plight a little more vividly than the average reader.

Just one day before our departure for Sicily we received a visit from Detective Chief Inspector Lewis of Swansea Police. He had been tasked with taking statements from the four defendants who have lodged complaints against the police,[57] and DC Cath Orford in particular, regarding their behaviour in their handling of *Operation Violet Oak*. Suing the police is expensive and unlikely to succeed, but if the same might also be said of making a complaint against them, the latter at least has the virtue of being free.

Each of us will have our own grievances, though there will be common threads running through all of them, centring around Cath Orford's communications with Florence which demonstrated a clear bias against us from the outset. Michael E will have questions to ask about the 'identity parade' in which Florence picked out his likeness unerringly, despite his insistence that the two had never met. He had handed over a picture of himself to Cath Orford which had been taken in the nineteen-nineties, and some weeks later included in a photo-lineup presented to Florence. What happened to that picture in the intervening weeks is a question Ms Orford will be required to answer.

I don't know exactly what issues his brother Eric will be concentrating on, though we can be sure Owen will be focussing, *inter alia,* on the 'photograph that never was'.[58] Simon C, unfortunately, will not be filing his own complaint. I talked to him recently, and he remains so traumatised by events he does

---

57 Although in a different division from Cardiff, Swansea is still part of South Wales Police. This of course raises questions of its own.

58 Florence has always insisted this photograph did exist, but has been unable to put her hand on it.

not feel he has the energy to take a complaint forward himself. This is a pity, because his treatment, with the police failing to examine his computer with its revelatory evidence, is perhaps the shabbiest of all. Still, we must respect his decision.

For my part, I spent the better part of three hours explaining where I feel the investigation went astray, from the beginning, with my being placed in handcuffs at Bristol Airport for no readily discernible reason, right through to the end, when Cath Orford persisted in 'counselling' Florence despite the furious protests of the lawyers at the Pre-Trial Review last November. Unfortunately, despite being given every opportunity to air my grievances, I forgot to mention an important point: that the police caved in very quickly after being told by Florence they could not interrogate her computer. If they had insisted, information thus gained might have given the defence vital information with which to challenge Florence on the stand, or even cause the CPS to drop the case before it got that far. What the hell. You can't remember everything.

DCI Lewis, who came over as a kindly, avuncular man, is clearly skilled in the art of placating complainants. In an atmosphere of deceptive coziness, he fielded all my comments with seeming infinite patience while his female assistant sat almost in silence, scribbling furiously in her notebook. He told us that there are four possible outcomes:

No case to answer. That DC Orford and the other officers will emerge unscathed, having been found to have done nothing wrong.

Poor Performance. In other words, that there are 'lessons to be learned' from the way the investigation was carried out, but no disciplinary action.

Misconduct. Possibly resulting in some sort of reprimand, and perhaps a censure appearing on an officer's permanent record.

Gross Misconduct. A severe reprimand, possibly a fine, and in the worst case scenario for them, dismissal.

DCI Lewis, despite his outward support of our position, remained tight-lipped about which way the decision might go, but both Liz (who was present at the interview) and I felt that the most likely final disposition will be number one, or at best two. All we can hope for is that behind closed doors, the police will be wondering what went so terribly wrong in this case, and how they might go about things better next time. On the other hand I wouldn't be surprised if they all simply commiserate with one another, and say something like:

"Shame really. It was all going so well until that package of wire thing."

"Yeah, that's what screwed us."

Given the change in attitude announced by Cressida Dick not so long ago, it is not beyond the realm of possibility that we are on the cusp of a new approach. But even if that is true, and I am by no means sure it is, I continue to be concerned about the hundreds of other cases similar to ours that are already in the system.

DCI Lewis finally informed us that the notes from the interview would be typed up, and a copy sent to us to approve. Given the complexity of the enquiry, he said, this process would be likely to take many months. And then, with warm handshakes all round, it was over and we were able to finish our packing.

Mark Crowley was delighted when I told him I had lodged a formal complaint against the police, but warned me against attempting to sue the police, the CPS or Florence herself. It would, he said, be an expensive folly, bound to be stressful and in all likelihood fail. His own view is that the police themselves should be taking action against Florence, either for perjury or perverting the course of justice, or both. But that is fantasy-land. The police turning on their own star witness? It's never going to happen. And while she has been proved to have been less than truthful on more than one occasion, Florence will doubtless stick to her story that she was horribly abused by the defendants until her dying day. Will she even now come up with fresh allegations against us? I wouldn't put it past her, but my team is confident she has taken things as far as she can, and the CPS will never again take more claims against us seriously. That is obviously a relief for us, though I worry about anyone else she may have encountered over the years. They are not safe. But for the moment, thank God, we are.

★

Wednesday the ninth of May 2018, four pm. I have just home from my regular midweek visit to my mother. Her twenty-four hour carers have now been installed for nearly four months and it is clear to everyone she is thriving under the new regime. Despite that, she never misses an opportunity to complain to me about them:

"I'm not master in my own house any more! They keep bullying me, telling me what to do all the time!"

I try to explain that they are there to help, that they were only brought in because she was losing the ability to look after herself. I invite her to consider how much happier she has been since they started working with her. And she agrees.

As custom dictates, I took her on a brief walk down to the sea, about a quarter of a mile from her house. In the week before we had left for Sicily we had enjoyed day after day of marvellous weather, but on our return home we found conditions had reverted to the unseasonable cold of early spring. Fortunately mother was well insulated against the cool blasts: quilted jacket, scarf, hat and gloves. Her legs, however, were covered only by stockings; not that she ever complains of the cold. She comes, as she likes to remind us, from the Derbyshire Dales, where they have "proper winters", and describe anyone who doesn't like the cold as "nesh".

Once on the beach we like to watch the tide as it rises or falls, and if it is near its height, watching its progression up, or down, a stone-built slipway. As it happened, we arrived at the precise moment of high tide. Standing just a foot back from the damp line marking its highest point, we waited for a few minutes to see if it had reached its limit, ready to dance backwards should it advance any further. But no, with each little wave it began slowly to recede. My mother said:

"Well, it's done very well to get this far, but now it's going away."

"Yes", I said. "Well done, sea."

And we both laughed.

On the way back up the gentle incline to her house, we watched the seagulls wheeling and cawing above our heads.

"One for sorrow, two for joy, three for a girl and four for a boy", she intoned.

In years gone by I would have reminded her that the rhyme relates to magpies, not seagulls, but there is no point now. She would forget what I said in less than a minute. She continued to stare at them a moment longer, and then remarked:

"Aren't they beautiful?"

I had to agree they were.

In recent months I have found her delight in such ordinary things puzzling, sometimes even faintly annoying. A seagull is beautiful, a daisy is beautiful, a puppy chasing a ball into the waves and then shaking itself is beautiful. So what?

But recent events have provided a new perspective for me. It is only when one's liberty has been threatened that the importance of life's minutiae are fully appreciated. As Jung Chang put it in *Wild Swans*:

'*When you are free, even plain water tastes sweet.*'

Today I am beginning to appreciate the beauty of small things once more. For me, now, they represent the very essence of freedom.

Afterword

2018 was a year of recovery for me. For the most part, it was a period of serenity, of quiet peace. Looking back at that time now, those days seem to glow with a kind of golden radiance. Sometimes I would wake with a feeling of dread, only to realise a moment later that I had nothing to fear, that everything was all right. I would give a great sigh of relief, and settle into enjoying my day. My body, however, took much longer to recover. My wife Liz predicted it would take a year for the stiffness and discomfort in my joints to dissipate completely, and she proved correct. Just when I was beginning to think they would never go away, they finally did, around the time of the first anniversary of our exoneration.

There was good news on the financial front as well. Both my barristers kindly agreed to revise their fees downwards, and Mark Crowley employed the services of a forensic accountant to analyse his own fees, item by item: every phone call, every piece of research, every case conference. They numbered in their hundreds. The accountant's fee in itself was substantial, but Crowley was able to use his findings to lobby the legal Aid Board to increase their offer. Without actually admitting it directly, they were forced in effect to concede their original offer had been grossly inadequate. Eventually my final bill came out at around £45,000. Still not exactly cheap, but a lot less than I had feared. Of course, had the case gone to trial, the bill would have been far in excess of £100,000. Which makes it another reason why I'm very glad it didn't.

As we finally waved goodbye to the 'Beast from the East', and the long, glorious summer of 2018 progressed, we waited for the results of the two investigations we had instigated: the complaint against South Wales Police over their handling of *Operation Violet Oak,* and a separate demand that the police charge Florence, like

Carl Beech, with fraud and attempting to pervert the course of justice. As the sun shone it was easy to persuade ourselves that either, or both, of these investigations might bear fruit.

Summer gave way to autumn, and then to winter before we heard anything. Then finally in November we were informed that the police would not be prosecuting Florence.

"...The investigation looked carefully at the question of whether any evidence could be presented to a jury that Florence lied to the original investigation team, and which could be proved beyond a reasonable doubt... Having spoken to all the police officers and crown prosecutors in the case it was felt that this evidential test was not met..."

Mark Crowley was furious on hearing the news.

"This is a disgrace! Evidential test? Rubbish! They're just afraid of being shown to be the dupes they were, and don't want to face any further embarrassment."

Disgrace or not, there was no appeal against this decision. We had to wear it. We had to wait a lot longer before hearing the result of our complaint against the police, but when it finally came in June 2019 it contained no surprises. Although the investigation found in our favour in one or two minor areas of 'poor performance', in general the police were exonerated in their actions. Once again my solicitor was incandescent in his condemnation of their findings:

"A whitewash, pure and simple! Of course, I must remind you I predicted this would happen from the outset."

Which he had.

In this case we were allowed to appeal its findings, and we each did so with some gusto. At first I was told my appeal had not addressed the issue using the correct template, though to be fair they did explain how do it according to their criteria. I re-wrote my appeal and a few weeks later was informed that the matter was at last going to be referred to the IOPC (Independent Office for Police Conduct). Mark Crowley warned me "Not to start celebrating just yet". Of course he was right to do so. In the Carl Beech case, the IOPC decided not to recommend disciplinary action against any of the police officers involved in *Operation Midland,* despite their mind-boggling credulity in believing every lie Beech told, however bizarre and outrageous it might have seemed to an outsider, even despite their disgraceful hounding of Leon Brittan who, at the time, was a very sick man. Finally in the last week of October 2019 we heard from the IOPC. It made for disappointing, if scarcely unexpected reading. While they acknowledged certain areas which they characterised as being to do with the 'poor performance' of some of the police officers, much of the blame, if there were any, lay at the door of the CPS. Mark Crowley called this a classic example of 'passing the parcel'.

In particular, the IOPC found no evidence that any officer had acted in an "intentionally reckless, dishonest or malicious manner". In consequence they failed to uphold *any* of the charges of misconduct made by the defendants. As far as I am aware, there is no appeal against this decision.

In a strange way I agree with them. Although the police can scarcely be said to have covered themselves in glory in their handling of Operation Violet Oak, no one acted with deliberate malice. And it is worth remembering that the real reason I nearly went to prison for the rest of my life for crimes I did not commit, was that someone went to the police and claimed I had committed a whole series of frightful atrocities against an innocent young girl.

To recap then, we shall be receiving no apology from the police, nor any compensation. This is not the case with Harvey Proctor, however, who has received both. I have wondered why the authorities see our cases so differently, but I suppose the answer is, Mr Proctor's accuser was found guilty of attempting to pervert the course of justice and sentenced to a lengthy term of imprisonment. My accuser, however, continues to walk free.

The way the police handle complaints of rape and sexual assault is beginning to change. In the spring of 2019 they announced they would from now on demand that complainants hand over their electronic devices for their scrutiny. This provoked a furious reaction from women's groups, who rightly saw it as an intrusion into victims' privacy. Despite this the policy has been rolled out across the country. It *is* an invasion of privacy, but it is the only way to get to the truth. Liam Allen, remember, was very nearly convicted of rape until text messages emerged that told a very different story from the one his accuser told the police. As it happens, I met him by chance at an *Innovations for Justice* meeting, and found him a charming young man, slim as a pencil, snappily dressed and possessing a lively, nervous intelligence. Interestingly, he told me that despite his acquittal, he still considered his reputation to have been destroyed. I found this odd, but then I am sixty-eight years old, my career behind me. He is in his twenties, with his whole life ahead of him. He is going to see things from a different perspective.

For centuries the justice system has been weighted heavily in favour of men. Then, following the revelations concerning Jimmy Savile and the advent of Alison Saunders at the head of the CPS, the balance began to shift towards women. But in early 2018, with Cressida Dick's announcement that the Met was giving up its policy of believing all complainants of sexual assault unquestioningly, and the police now insisting on examining complainants' devices, it seemed to me that the 'pendulum of justice' was gradually moving back towards the centre.

In September 2019, however, a report was published[59] which showed that while complaints of rape and sexual assault had reached an all-time high, convictions were at a record *low*. The reasons for this are complex and the subject of passionate debate, but you don't have to be a legal expert to see that there is something terribly wrong with this picture. To me one fact remains inescapable: even as we approach the third decade of the third Millennium, the goal of achieving true justice for both men and women remains elusive.

Steve Glascoe
December 2019

---

59 Home Office: Crime Outcomes, England and Wales, 2018-2019

Acknowledgements

My legal team:

Christopher Clee, QC, leading counsel, Susan Ferrier, junior counsel, Mark Crowley, lead solicitor, Samantha Day, Jonathan Webb, solicitors, Alistair Coxhead, police station legal representative, Alex Wade, legal advisor.

And Victoria Simon-Shore, specialist legal advisor.

My friends:

These wonderful people stood by me from the outset, demonstrating unswerving and unqualified loyalty. They are, quite simply, gold:

Paul Barrett, Paul and Beverly Beauchamp, Tracy and Rob Brazier, Debbie Coburn, Linda Gibbs, Philip Glascoe, Martin and Jenny Greenwood, Richard Gwyn, Mo and Harry Holland, Lynette Jones, Dr Suzanne Jordan, Diana and Peter Morgan, The Reads, Carol, Martin, James and Helen, The Relphs, Paul, Terry, Lorna and Matthew, Suzanne Shepherd, Barbara Southard, Dr Alan Stone, Ali Williams, Steve and Louise Young.

My publisher, Mick Felton, and his support team. He believed in the worth of my project from the beginning, and without that you would not be reading this book now.